Building Parent Engagement in Schools

Larry Ferlazzo
&
Lorie Hammond

Linworth Books

LIBRARIES UNLIMITED
An Imprint of ABC-CLIO, LLC

A B C ☙ C L I O

Santa Barbara, California • Denver, Colorado • Oxford, England

Library of Congress Cataloging-in-Publication Data
Ferlazzo, Larry.
  Building parent engagement in schools / Larry Ferlazzo & Lorie Hammond.
    p. cm.
  Includes bibliographical references and index.
  ISBN-13: 978-1-58683-342-8 (pbk.); 978-1-58683-405-0 (ebook)
  ISBN-10: 1-58683-342-1 (pbk.); 1-58683-405-3 (ebook)
  1. Education--Parent participation--Case studies. 2. Motivation in education--United
States--Case studies. 3. Academic achievement--United States--Case studies. I.
Hammond, Lorie A. II. Title.
  LB1048.5.F47 2009
  371.19'2--dc22   2009002310

13 12 11 10 9   1 2 3 4 5

This book is also available on the World Wide Web as an eBook.
Visit www.abc-clio.com for details.

ABC-CLIO, LLC
130 Cremona Drive, P.O. Box 1911
Santa Barbara, California 93116-1911

This book is printed on acid-free paper ∞

Manufactured in the United States of America

Table of Contents

Table of Figures

About the Authors

Larry Ferlazzo has taught English and Social Studies at Luther Burbank High School in Sacramento for five years. Prior to becoming a teacher he spent twenty years working as a community organizer assisting low- and moderate-income families improve their communities. He has won numerous awards, including the Leadership for a Changing World award from the Ford Foundation, the International Reading Association Presidential Award for Reading and Technology, and the Sacramento State College of Education's "Education Partnership Award." He writes a blog for teachers about working with English Language Learners (http://larryferlazzo.edublogs.org/) and also has a website for students (http://larryferlazzo.com/).

Lorie Hammond, Ph. D., is a professor of Teacher Education at California State University at Sacramento. She has been a teacher educator in diverse, urban schools for the past eleven years, and has created school community gardens and professional development schools. Lorie's background is in science, art, and bilingual education, and in doing oral history projects with teachers and parents based on the funds of knowledge held by immigrant communities. Prior to teaching at the university, Lorie was a newcomer teacher, a district bilingual science coordinator, and a gifted and talented teacher. She has published widely on socially relevant science education, and is currently starting a private non-profit school called the Peregrine Project. For more information contact lhammond@csus.edu or http://theperegrineproject.net/.

Acknowledgments

Larry Ferlazzo

I'd like to thank my wife, Jan, and my children and grandchildren--Stacia (and her husband, Rich), Nik, Karli, Shea, and Ava--who have helped me see and experience the importance of parent engagement in education. In addition, I'd like to thank the administrators, faculty, staff, parents, and students of Luther Burbank High School for helping me learn about its same value from a teacher's perspective. I'd also like to express my appreciation to Kate Vande Brake and Cyndee Anderson from Linworth Publishing for their help and support in developing this manuscript. Lastly, I'd like to recognize my collaborator and co-author, Lorie Hammond.

Lorie Hammond, PhD

For my part, I would also like to thank my partner, George, and my children, their spouses, and grandchildren, Elena, Joe, Eli, Fernanda, Alex, Rebecca, Liam, and Sammy, who make all endeavors worthwhile. I would also like to thank my university, CSU Sacramento, and Pia Wong, the Equity Network, for supporting the school-community garden project, and the student teachers for all their service learning work; our school district partners and the wonderful teachers in Washington Unified School District; Maggie de Leon, Director of the International Studies Project and Cyndi Thompson, Director of FELP; our community partners including Sr. Cora Salazar of FISH, Deb Bruns of the Yolo County Office of Education and Barbara Merino and Joyce Gutstein of UC Davis; and the garden coordinators, Liew Saetern, Alicia and Ernesto Mendez and Alice Peralta, and Imelda Subia Smith; and especially the immigrant communities in West Sacramento who grew the beautiful and productive gardens.

Introduction

The Purpose of This Book

It is well established that meaningful parent engagement in children's educations increases student achievement. For this reason, *No Child Left Behind* and other federal and state mandates encourage schools to engage with parents and community members. For many teachers, administrators, librarians, and other staff members at schools, finding time in a busy work schedule to meet with parents can seem overwhelming. This book proposes a paradigm shift: a new way of looking at the roles which staff members and parents play in schools. By "engaging" parents as active players in the school community, rather than "involving" them in school-centered projects, school staff members can be energized rather than exhausted by their relationships to their communities. Our goal is to show educators that if they base community engagement on issues which motivate parents in authentic ways, and help them develop the power to act, then parents and community members can actually make school staff members' jobs easier rather than harder.

This book is written as a handbook which illustrates simple steps which can be used to engage any community. The projects described have been carried out successfully by the two authors of the book, and have worked in a variety of challenging communities, including various minority and immigrant communities. The same approach would work with mainstream communities as well. It is our sincere hope that our readers will be able to engage parents in their school settings as a means of improving student success, and that this book can be a practical guide for beginning the process.

How This Book Is Organized

This book is organized around a single approach, which can be applied to any situation. This approach, which we call "parent engagement," is described in chapter one, by being contrasted to a more traditional approach, which we call "parent involvement." The key to parent engagement is to build upon the social capital, or the natural needs, strength, and knowledge which any community has, and to mobilize parents as active participants in solving the problems which they and their children encounter. Parent engagement is a long-term relationship between a school and its community, with the general goal of improving the social capital, and hence the efficacy and academic achievement of that community over time.

Chapters two through five each illustrate successful projects that schools have accomplished with a community of students and their families. The authors have either been directly or indirectly connected to each one. Each project is written in the same format, so that the elements of parent engagement described in chapter one are illustrated in the context of each project. Each chapter begins with a parable, then moves into the story of how a particular project was organized successfully in a certain school community, and how it resulted in improved student achievement. Chapters cover a range of topics: home visits, family literacy through a home computer project, school-community gardens, and organizing communities to address problems that they face.

Our purpose is to illustrate how the reader's school might do a project like those outlined, or more importantly, how the principles illustrated through these projects can be applied to any school community.

Parent Engagement and Standards

Research has shown the connection between parent engagement in schools and student achievement. Each of the projects developed in the chapters of this book increased student achievement, as is described in the chapters themselves.

How to Use This Book

All readers should read chapter one, which lays out the framework of parent engagement, the central message of this book. This framework can be used to approach any parent community. The other chapters provide examples of how this framework acts itself out in a variety of circumstances. Readers might choose to read chapters 2-5 in any order, although chapter 5, which deals with how to organize a parent community to solve social problems, has general applications of value to all readers.

Who Will Benefit from This Book?

This book is designed for a broad audience of education professionals, including teachers, school librarians, community outreach workers, administrators, and more. It is also designed to be useful to anyone interested in engaging communities in schools, such as school board members or PTA leaders, and for pre-service teachers who want to learn about home-school relationships.

This book is written in an informal, story-telling style which makes it a quick and easy read for busy professionals who need action more than words. A comprehensive list of resources is provided at the end of the book on all of the topics considered, so that interested professionals can link with more specific sources.

CHAPTER 1

What Is Parent Engagement?

THE JAY AND THE PEACOCK

A jay venturing into a yard where peacocks used to walk, found there a number of feathers which had fallen from the peacocks when they were molting. He tied them all to his tail and strutted down towards the peacocks. When he came near them they soon discovered the cheat, and striding up to him pecked at him and plucked away his borrowed plumes. So the jay could do no better than go back to the other jays, who had watched his behavior from a distance; but they were equally annoyed with him, and told him:

> *"It is not only fine feathers that make fine birds."*
> Aesop's Fables <http://www.pacificnet.net/~johnr/aesop/>

This fable is about a bird who thought that a few feathers could make him be something he was not. This book is about why and how it is in schools' self-interest to have a parent *engagement* strategy that does not settle at having a few parents on a school site council, or even a large number coming to a Back-to-School night. This book is about providing specific ways that schools can avoid the same trap as the jay. Tempting as it may be, and as challenging as it may be to do more, a few parents (or even many of them) coming to a meeting or periodically turning-out large numbers of parents to a school event and *calling it* parent engagement does not *make it* an effective parent engagement strategy.

School administrators, teachers, librarians, and staff have plenty on their plate right now. The point of this book is not to add a great deal more on it. Instead, it is to show that, with varying degrees of effort— large or small—schools can get a "bigger bang for their (figurative) buck" in terms of increased student academic achievement by being strategic in *engaging,* as opposed to *involving* parents and the community (though this contrast draws from a framework originally developed in the 1990's by the Industrial Areas Foundation as part of their organizing work in the Texas public schools, and from the work of Boston College Professor Dennis Shirley in his book *Community Organizing For Urban School Reform* (70-76), the authors of this book want to emphasize that the description found here is not necessarily using a paradigm that is exactly the same). The point of *engaging* parents in school is to assist them in developing and harnessing their own energy. The point is not to demand that school staff dig much deeper into their own already stressed energy reserves. This book lays-out guidelines and suggestions for how school staff can be strategic in engaging parents, and how they might want to look at their present roles a bit differently. All staff can play a part, and perhaps school librarians, because of their slightly flexible schedule, their knowledge of curriculum and students at all grades, and their special expertise in literacy, can play a particularly key one.

By engaging parents and the communities in which they are located, public schools can reconnect to the Latin roots of the word "public," which means "open to all in the community." Through being intentional about connecting to parents, schools can also more effectively meet the "letter of the law" in the *No Child Left Behind Act* that requires schools to develop and implement a parent involvement plan. By *engaging* with parents, schools can recognize that, to paraphrase the English poet John Donne, "no school is an island." Education writer and researcher Richard Rothstein has pointed out that it is possible for schools to *narrow* the achievement gap without responding to issues outside the schoolhouse walls, but that it will not be possible to *close* it without making that connection. http://www.epi.org/webfeatures/viewpoints/200608_rothstein_finn/rothstein-response_to_finn.pdf

This chapter and book is more of a compass, not a road map. It will offer some guidelines/criteria to consider when exploring what kind of relationships schools can have with parents. The rest of the book will provide specific examples of projects that can be undertaken which meet the "engagement" criteria, including the Parent/Teacher Home Visiting Project, school/community gardens, a home computer family literacy project, and working with community organizing groups. Ultimately, the question is "Can parent engagement be one way that will help teachers, school staff, and administrators (and, of course, parents) achieve their goals, particularly increasing student academic achievement?"

The purpose of this book is not to say that teachers and administrators who are pursuing parent *involvement* are doing something bad—they are not. In fact, it would be difficult to find any typical parent involvement activities (volunteering in the classroom, helping with school fundraisers, participating in Back-To-School and Open House nights, etc.) that would do anything but be beneficial to students. They could also be a step towards parent *engagement*. The purpose of this book is to suggest that a parent *engagement* strategy might result in much bigger gains for students, their parents, the school, and the community. To paraphrase an old community organizer's axiom: Parent involvement may provide opportunities to enhance student achievement, but parent engagement might provide *superior* opportunities.

As Debbie Pushor, a Canadian professor who has written about parent involvement/engagement efforts in a somewhat similar way has said, "It's not about blaming. It is about saying, 'Stop and let's pay attention. Let's really look at it and say 'Is this what we want?'" (Pushor <Edtech Talk Webcast; Parents as Partners, May 5th, 2008, http://edtechtalk.com/node/3161>)

What Does Research Show About the Effect of Engaging/Involving Parents on Student Achievement?

Countless studies have found explicit connections between increased academic student achievement and parent participation. *A New Wave of Evidence: The Impact of School, Family, and Community Connections on Student Achievement*, written by the Southwest

Educational Development Laboratory in 2002, analyzed 51 studies, and all but two were published from 1995 to 2002. The analysis found that the benefits for students included:

- Higher grade point averages and scores on standardized tests
- Enrollment in more challenging academic programs
- More classes passed and credits earned
- Better attendance
- Improved behavior at home and at school
- Better social skills and adaptation to school (Southwest Educational Development Laboratory 24)

It should also be pointed out that William H. Jeynes, in his own meta-analysis of 52 studies of parent involvement, found that many of the same improvements in student achievement resulted across all races (Jeynes 102).

In addition, case studies in the following chapters will discuss how each particular example of engaging parents is research-based and has been linked to student achievement.

What Is the Difference Between Parent *Involvement* and Parent *Engagement* and How Can They Be Assessed?

Merriam Webster's Dictionary defines involvement as "to enfold or envelop." It defines engagement as "to interlock with; to mesh." Those definitions get to the crux of the difference. When schools *involve* parents they are leading with their institutional self-interest and wants—school staff are leading with their *mouths*. When schools *engage* parents they are leading with the parents' self-interests (their wants and dreams) in an effort to develop a genuine partnership—school staff are leading with their *ears*. Debbie Pushor has described the difference in similar ways (Pushor 2).

This book is making a clear distinction between engaging and involving. It should be pointed out that many, if not most, of the other literature on parents and school tend to use the terms interchangeably.

Because of that, it is very difficult to separate and identify assessments that show which (using the definitions that are used in this book) have been more effective in increasing student achievement.

However, some data does provide indications that parent engagement, as defined in this book, might be particularly fruitful. Studies highlighted in the 2002 Southwest Education Development Laboratory (SEDL) study referred to earlier (a subsequent 2008 SEDL analysis of 31 studies done between 2005 and 2008 "reinforc[ed the] previous research findings" [Ferguson et al., 5]) pointed out the importance of some of the criteria we use to define parent engagement as described below.

- **PARENT/TEACHER RELATIONSHIPS:**

The development of quality parent-to-teacher relationships and quality teacher-to-teacher relationships are critical to school success. "…social trust—the quality of the relationships—is the key factor associated with improving schools" (SEDL 43). A key way for schools to develop these kinds of relationships is for staff to "understand and relate to [families'] needs" (SEDL 66). "When school staff engage in caring and trusting relationships with parents that recognize parents as partners in the educational development of children, these relationships enhance parents' desire to be involved and influence how they participate in their children's educational development" (SEDL 45).

- **PARENT INVITATIONS AND ROLES:**

How parents are invited to participate in the life of the school, and into what roles, is a question schools need to ask themselves. "Effective programs to engage families and community embrace a philosophy of partnership. The responsibility for children's educational development is a collaborative enterprise among parents, school staff, and community members" (SEDL 51).

- **DECISION-MAKING POWER:**

The higher parents' sense of efficacy, their sense of power to influence and get things accomplished, such as having "a positive impact such as improving quality of the school and making the neighborhood a better place….then the more their children reported doing better in school and feeling happy, safe, and stable" (SEDL 33).

Let's now examine more in-depth how this book's parent engagement criteria can develop these and other strategies to increase student achievement.

FIGURE 1.1 Beginning the Process

	INVOLVEMENT	ENGAGEMENT
Whose energy drives it? Who initiates it?	Ideas and energy come from the schools and government mandates. Schools try to "sell" their ideas to parents. School staff and public institutions might feel they know what the problems are and how to fix them, and determine the criteria to use in evaluating success.	Ideas are elicited from parents by school staff in the context of developing trusting relationships. They emerge from parent/community needs and priorities. More parent energy drives the efforts.
What is the invitation?	Parents might be *irritated*—pushed to do something about what staff might perceive as important, and asked to do things without necessarily having a trusting and reciprocal relationship with school staff.	Parents are *agitated*—they are challenged to do something about what they feel is important to them. Staff learn what is important through developing a relationship.

It is one thing for school staff to approach parents and ask them to participate in a fundraising event or help paint the athletic field, or to invite them to sit on a school site council, and then, if they don't necessarily receive an overwhelmingly positive response, to feel discouraged that parents don't seem to be interested in helping the school. It's an entirely different matter when parents are asked about their hopes and dreams for the future—for their children and for themselves—then asked what ideas they have about how they and the school can best help achieve them.

A question sometimes asked of new community organizers by their mentors/trainers is: "Have you ever called people apathetic when they don't come to our meetings to talk about the things we want them to talk about? That's being a bad organizer." In other words, organizers who focus on what they, the organizers, want are often unsuccessful. They tend to blame that lack of success on what they sometimes call apathy in others.

This can be called the "irritating" approach, one that tends to cause displeasure, annoyance, and frustration to the people organizers are trying to encourage to participate in public life. It is also discouraging to the organizer. Irritation is viewed as leading with what the organizer wants as opposed to listening to the wants of others.

This would be contrasted with an "agitational" approach, one that would, as various dictionaries define the word, "arouse interest" with the goal of "putting things into motion ..."

Agitation is viewed as challenging people to reflect on their own lives and experiences and their visions for themselves and for their families. In other words, the focus is on people's self-interests.

If we talk "with (not to) parents" (Sarason 11) and ask parents to share their concerns, we might find that they are concerned about the following:

- the lack of activities for their children after school and before they get home from work

- their desire to develop more of their own skills so they can get a better-paying job to help their child pay for college

- their frustration at not being able to make "ends meet"

- their wanting to have the neighborhood be a safer place so they don't have to worry about crime affecting their families

- their interest in learning about their rights as immigrants and wanting help on a path towards citizenship

- their worries about not being able to afford to have family members go to the doctor when they are ill.

It should also be pointed out that many "self-interests" are difficult to accomplish on one's own, and require working with others to succeed.

Schools, and their staff, who show that they are interested in learning and helping on these issues might be pleased at the potential results. Not only can schools assist parents connect to other parents and community institutions who share the same concerns and help them develop effective solutions that would be more likely driven by parent energy, but parents are also then more likely to want to hear and act on suggestions from the school about how they can better support their child's learning at home. Who are you more likely to want to listen to—someone who tells you what you should do, or generally only contacts you when there's a problem or task to be dealt with, or someone who tries to build a reciprocal relationship?

In addition, as parents develop more self-confidence in responding to their own concerns, it is not unreasonable to believe that this same self-confidence can spill over to providing additional support to their child's academic life.

FIGURE 1.2 Roles of Parents and School Staff

	INVOLVEMENT	ENGAGEMENT
What is the role of the parent?	He is a volunteer who is generally directed by school staff towards completing tasks or a client who receives services and information.	She is considered a *leader* (or a *potential* leader) who is integral to identifying a vision and goals. She encourages others to contribute their own vision to that big picture and helps perform the tasks that need to be achieved to reach those goals.
What is the role of the teacher/school librarian?	She is more of a social worker who might do things for the parents, or tends to tell them what they should be doing with their child.	He is more of an *organizer* who helps parents do things for themselves, and elicits from parents ideas about what the parents and school staff could be doing to better help their child and their community.
What is the role of the administrator?	Develops the vision and assigns tasks to parents to help accomplish them.	Encourages parents and staff to help develop a joint vision, and helps develop those leadership abilities, while recognizing that tasks are just a tool towards that end.

First, it is important to clarify that the roles listed on the chart are not always either one or the other. They sometimes merge, and depending on the situation and the particular parent, sometimes involvement makes more sense. When it comes time to help with their child's prom night, some parents might want to just be told what to do and when to do it! The real question is about which role you *tend* to take—which side do you operate on *most* of the time?

Parents have an incredible amount of wisdom, experience, knowledge, relationships, and potential power—much of which is untapped by schools.

This book is not necessarily advocating parents consulting with teachers and administrators on how to teach the curriculum, though the authors have had these kinds of conversations and felt they have become better teachers as a result. It is suggesting, though, that schools and their staff can …

- … actively seek to learn the concerns and hopes of families (through a variety of means—surveys followed-up by personal contact, home visits, discussions during Open House) and not just focus exclusively on what is happening with their child/student.

- … assist parents in connecting with others (both other parents and other community institutions) who share similar concerns and enforce what the Industrial Areas Foundation (the largest community organizing network in the United States) calls the "Iron Rule: Never do for others what they can do for themselves. Never." School staff can elicit and give suggestions for action, and provide support, encouragement, and advice on how parents can pursue their goals, but the primary energy needs to come from the parents themselves.

- … look for opportunities when parents can use their "Funds of Knowledge" (what they know and have experienced) to enrich academic instruction and learning—both in and out of the classroom. An excellent lesson that occurred one day at Luther Burbank High School in Sacramento was when a pre-literate and non-English-speaking parent of a student came in and showed how he could repair and play an extraordinarily beautiful and complex Hmong musical instrument. The ESL class spent days afterward writing, reading, speaking, and developing a slideshow about the experience—all in English.

- … take advantage of the vast years of experience parents have with their children and go to them for counsel on how their children learn best.

FIGURE 1.3 Purpose, Decision-Making, and Partnerships

	INVOLVEMENT	ENGAGEMENT
What is the Purpose?	Support students by strengthening and assisting school programs and priorities.	Support students by developing parent relationships, strengthening families, and improving their local communities.
Decision-Making Power	School staff might look at power as a finite "pie"--if parents get some, then schools lose some. Staff are the experts.	There is recognition that more possibilities are created when more stakeholders have power to make real decisions--the "pie" itself gets bigger. Parents are recognized as co-educators and experts in their own right.
What kinds of partnerships are developed?	"Narrow & Shallow." Schools might get gift certificates from businesses, or staff might initiate bringing social services to school sites with minimal parent input. Police, for example, are brought in to deal with campus safety issues only.	"Broad & Deep." Technical assistance is provided by community groups and universities on leadership development and other issues parents identify. Partnerships are developed with businesses, the police, local political bodies, and other entities to respond to community-wide issues.

Social service organizations often have a single and noble purpose—they might be focused on developing affordable housing for low-income families, or providing job opportunities, or on responding to any number of other social ills.

 A community organizing group might be much more successful than these groups in delivering concrete neighborhood improvements in the areas of housing, jobs, etc. Why? Because they are more often focused on investing in mutual *relationships* with a much broader group of people.

Though it might seem counter-intuitive to some, a similar perspective can work for schools.

As famed educational reformer John Dewey wrote in 1939:

> I might also say that it is surprising how many alleged pedagogical problems relating to such matters as 'discipline and freedom, motivation,' etc. either vanish or are greatly reduced when a school is a living part of the community. (Dewey in Clapps X)

What Is Social Capital and What Does It Have to Do with Schools?

The word "capital" has many meanings. Physical capital refers to the tools and equipment necessary for industrial production. Economic capital is money. Human capital is the training and education that people receive so they can become economically productive. The term *social capital* became popularized by Robert Putnam's book *Bowling Alone*. He defined it as the value generated by the "connections among individuals—social networks and the norms of reciprocity and trustworthiness that arise from them" (Putnam 19). Beliefs and shared expectations of behavior are also shared this way. This, of course, is a key result of an effective parent engagement strategy.

Putman identified the importance of developing social capital for all aspects of a healthy society in the 1990's. However, both the originator of the concept and a key researcher on it prior to Putman directly connected school's promoting social capital with student academic achievement.

L.J. Hanifan, a state supervisor of rural public schools in West Virginia, first coined the phrase *social capital* in 1916 as he promoted a strategy eerily similar to the parent engagement criteria discussed in this chapter. He cited numerous improvements as a result, including increased student attendance. After writing about the parent engagement work of one school district, he concludes:

> I am firmly convinced that the supervisor and teachers, whose achievements I have described, have struck bed-rock in community building. It is not what they did for the people that counts for most in what was achieved; it was what they led the people to do for themselves that was really important. Tell the people what they ought to do, and they will say in effect, 'Mind your own business.' But help them to discover for themselves what ought to be done and they will not be satisfied until it is done. First the people must get together. Social capital must be accumulated. Then community improvements may begin. The more the people do for themselves the larger will community social capital become, and the greater will be the dividends upon the social investment. (138)

Sociologist James Coleman in the 1980's connected higher high school graduation rates to the social capital generated between school staff, students, and parents (Coleman 1988). A more recent study by Leana and Pil, published in 2006, called "Social Capital and Organizational Performance: Evidence From Urban Public Schools," examined 88 public schools. It found a "causal" relationship between what it called "external social capital" (relationships between the school and parents and others) and student reading achievement. (Leana and Pil 2006).

The Consortium on Chicago School Research in 1995 surveyed staff at 210 schools. Whereas teachers at the academically most highly-rated thirty schools said they felt like they had a very positive relationship with parents and that they cared about the community where the school was located, survey results from staff at the bottom thirty schools were the polar opposite on both points (Sebring, Bryk, Easton 61).

An effective parent engagement strategy can result in improved student achievement through the social capital it builds, and through the self-confidence and leadership skills that parents develop through their participation.

In addition, some concrete community improvements that could be gained by assisting families act on their concerns, hopes, and dreams can have a positive effect on student achievement as well.

How Can Community Improvement Directly Impact Student Achievement?

In 1966 Professor James Coleman, the same researcher who documented the effect of social capital on high school graduation rates, completed a Congressionally-mandated study analyzing why students in low-income communities did worse in school than middle-class children. His landmark study concluded that the background and resources of the families were the primary causes for the disparity. Richard Rothstein from the Economic Policy Institute and former national education columnist for *The New York Times* has written extensively about the limited success schools can have in eliminating this achievement gap without other community improvements occurring (Rothstein 2004). Rothstein highlights issues around housing, health, jobs, and economic security concerns—concerns which are ones that may often come up in conversations with parents.

- Rothstein points out that a lack of affordable housing makes lower-income families tend to have to move more often. Switching schools in midyear can hurt the academic progress of students and their new classmates (135).

Schools can work with parents to develop or maintain long-term affordable housing. For example, the Sacramento Mutual Housing Association cooperated with a school and their parents to build 70 affordable units near the school. Schools can also work with community groups to organize "housing fairs" on-site to provide information on local housing opportunities.

- Rothstein also writes that the lack of adequate health care can result in problems that affect learning, including hearing and vision problems, as well as untreated dental issues whose pain affects student concentration in class (37).

By engaging parents, schools can work with them to ensure that their children are enrolled in their state's Child Insurance Program, as well as help parents organize for local accessible and affordable clinics (on or off-campus). Additionally, students can help parents combat the increased environmental hazards prevalent in low-income communities. For example, schools and religious congregations worked together to stop a hazardous waste incinerator from being opened across the street from a school in Los Angeles.

- Rothstein highlights that because of lower-paying jobs and less "wealth," lower-income families often do not have the same amount of assets for providing increased educational opportunities for their children, such as books, computers, travel opportunities, and enrichment classes. In fact, he shares studies that have shown that this is a problem even when ethnic minority families and white families have similar incomes, since the ethnic minority families tend to have had the higher incomes for a much smaller amount of time (133).

Schools can help parents organize wealth creation efforts, such as Individual Development Accounts (IDAs). IDAs are a growing effort by non-profit groups using private and public resources to combine financial education with a savings program. Program participants' savings are matched (ranging from 1-1 to 5-1) and the combined savings can typically be used to help purchase a home, pay for education-related expenses, or to start a business. Parents and school staff could have programs provide the trainings on school sites. Economic status is also related to legal residency and citizenship. Schools can also help parents who identify that as a concern to organize citizenship classes on campus.

> **Schools can also help parents who identify that as a concern to organize citizenship classes on-campus.**

Obviously, even with the most effective parent engagement strategy, schools alone do not have sufficient power to move public policy towards making affordable housing, accessible health care, and increased economic opportunities available to all low-income families. However, schools, by working with parents and with other institutions that also comprise what is called Civil Society (small business associations, religious congregations, neighborhood and non-profit groups, labor unions) can play a role in making important incremental steps towards achieving these goals and the resulting increase in student academic achievement. Taking these actions is one way they can stop being what education author Seymour Sarason calls an "encapsulated school" (19). The final chapter in this book will describe some of these potential collaborations in more detail.

CHAPTER 2

Home Visits

THE CROW AND THE PITCHER

A Crow, half-dead with thirst, came upon a Pitcher which had once been full of water; but when the Crow put its beak into the mouth of the Pitcher he found that only very little water was left in it, and that he could not reach far enough down to get at it. He tried, and he tried, but at last had to give up in despair. Then a thought came to him, and he took a pebble and dropped it into the Pitcher. Then he took another pebble and dropped it into the Pitcher. Then he took another pebble and dropped that into the Pitcher. Then he took another pebble and dropped it into the Pitcher….At last, at last, he saw the water mount up near him, and after casting in a few more pebbles he was able to quench his thirst and save his life.

"Little by little does the trick."
Aesop's Fables <http://www.pacificnet.net/~johnr/aesop/>

T he Crow was faced with a problem—he needed to get the water at the bottom of the pitcher. He could have taken the easy way out and knocked the pitcher over, but, if he had done that, he probably would only have gotten a very tiny amount before it spilled out onto the ground. Instead of choosing the strategy of doing a little work for a little "pay-off," he chose to demonstrate patience and work methodically so he could get as much water as possible.

Schools, in their parent *involvement* efforts, will settle sometimes to get *who they can* (a handful of parents) instead of *who they want* (large numbers of parents). Teachers and other staff making personal home visits—one at a time—over a lengthy period, can be successful in *engaging* larger numbers of parents.

Of course, teachers making visits to the homes of their students is not a particularly new or unusual idea—it's a practice some teachers have done for years. Many times, though, these home visits are done when there is a particular, and major, problem that has arisen affecting the student.

This chapter, however, is going to focus on schools that have made these kinds of home visits a systematic process with the help of the nationally-acclaimed Parent/Teacher Home Visit Project (PTHVP). The focus of these visits is not to tell the parent about a problem with their child and prescribe a solution. Instead, the emphasis is on the teacher developing a *relationship* with the parents.

What Is the Background of the Parent/Teacher Home Visit Project?

Sacramento Area Congregations Together (ACT) is a group of churches, synagogues, and neighborhood groups that is part of PICO, a national network of groups that utilize community organizing to improve neighborhoods (this book's fifth chapter will share more extensively about community organizing). In 1998, after conversations within their congregations, ACT members in South Sacramento, a lower-income community, decided they wanted to do something about their area's public schools. They then began a series of individual meetings, focus groups, and research actions to explore potential strategies to pursue.

What they discovered was what then ACT staff-person and now Executive Director of the Parent/Teacher Home Visit Project, Carrie Rose, described as a "cycle of blame." "Teachers were working hard and parents were working hard, but no one was communicating and, instead, they were blaming each other" (Rose in conversation 2008). As Rose described in a DVD about the project:

In our school district, like most urban school districts, teachers drive in and drive out—they don't live in the neighborhood in which they teach. So there are a lot of assumptions and a lot of fears that they build about the neighborhood. Likewise, the parents, families, and community members tend to build a lot of assumptions about the teachers when they see them driving in and driving out. (Rose 2006)

ACT did find some parents who had good relationships with teachers and found in several cases it was due to home visits that had been made. James Keddy from PICO says that this discovery then "led to a discussion about what would happen if half the teachers in a school were involved in home visits" (Keddy in *The Parent Home Visiting Project* DVD, 2006).

Meetings with leaders of the local teacher's union and the Sacramento School District led to the development of a unique home visiting model that included three key elements:

1. Home visits would be voluntary, but teachers would need to be paid for their time.

2. Training would be required before teachers went out on the visits.

3. Leadership for the project would be provided by three partners: parents from ACT, the teacher's union, and the school district.

The three partners shared the perspective of Cory Jones, a second-grade teacher who was an early leader of the project:

With a great curriculum, with a great teacher, if you leave out the home … your results for that particular student are going to be a little low. In the inner city schools, lots of the students aren't reaching the standards. It's probably because one of those three key players is not in the ball game. (Jones in *The Parent Home Visiting Project* DVD, 2006)

With financial support from the teacher's union and the School District, and utilizing various federal and state grants the Parent/Teacher Home Visit Project was created with three equal partners: ACT, the Sacramento City Unified School District, and The Sacramento City Teachers Association. They began in 1999 to see what they could do about strengthening the "home" part of the "ball game."

How Did the Parent/Teacher Home Visit Project Begin?

The home-visiting project began in 1999 in eight schools—six elementary and two middle (seventh and eighth grade). The visits were voluntary for family and school staff members. Several important components were in place by that time.

TRAINING WORKSHOP:

First, all partners agreed that teachers would be required to participate in a four-hour training prior to being eligible for the stipends they would be paid for the visits. Teachers, as part of the union contract in the Sacramento Unified School District, were required to take eighteen hours of professional development workshops each school year, and the three hour training, if teachers chose to take it, would be considered part of those eighteen hours.

The training was, and is, considered critical to the success of the project. These workshops typically occur at the school site. Jointly led by parents and teachers, the training helps teachers develop clarity about the primary purpose of the home visits—to build a relationship. Role-plays during the training accentuate that message. The PTHVP (Parent/Teacher Home Visit Project) believes that only after a trusting relationship is developed can issues of accountability and tasks be meaningfully discussed. The training also reviews practical details to help ensure the visit is a success.

These details include calling parents in advance to set up an appointment to visit, explaining their purpose, learning if a translator will be needed, and making sure parents know if anyone will be accompanying the teacher (the PTHVP recommends that two staff go on each visit). Teachers are encouraged to make a reminder call the day before the visit.

Next is the visit itself. Teachers and other participating school staff are encouraged to try to "check their assumptions at the door" as much as possible—putting aside cultural stereotypes and prejudices, whatever they might believe about the family based on their experience with the child, their impressions about the neighborhood, etc.

In beginning the visit, particularly because for many parents the expectation is that a teacher would not be visiting them if there was not a problem with their child, the PTHVP suggests teacher's start off emphasizing that they are there "to get to know you better and let you know that we care about (student's name) ... [and] work together to ensure that (student's name) has a successful year" (*PTHVP Training Manual*). It's also good if teachers can begin sharing positive comments about the student, if the visit is being done after the school year has begun.

Next, the teacher would ask questions to get to know the parents: What brought you to this community? Do you have other children in school? What was your school experience as a child? Since these visits are not "interviews" and building a relationship is a reciprocal undertaking, teachers are also encouraged to share their own personal story as well. For example, they can share what led them to become an educator.

One way to make sure that the visit is not perceived as an interview is not to take notes. The PTHVP believes that not only does the act of note-taking take away from it being seen by the parent as a genuine relationship-building visit, it also takes away from the ability of the teacher to concentrate on engaging in a two-way conversation. In addition, active note-taking is a staple of visitors from a number of other public agencies that might have more negative connotations in the parent's eyes, such as Child Protective Services, the local police, etc. Of course, notes can be written down immediately after the visit in the teacher's car.

These conversations, in addition to helping develop a relationship, can contribute to teachers gaining a better understanding of the "funds of knowledge" present in their students' families. "Funds of knowledge" <http://www.learnnc.org/lp/pages/939> are the skills, background, culture, and experience that a family, and a student, can contribute to their learning and the learning of others. This understanding can help teachers develop lessons that better connect to students' prior knowledge, and consider ways to invite parents to assist in the student learning process.

Teachers are also encouraged to ask questions that would specifically help them be a better teacher to the child: What seems to give their child the most energy? When has he/she seemed to do best in school? What advice would you give a teacher of your child?

Parents are also asked about their hopes and dreams, both for their individual child and their entire families. It's suggested that teachers, too, share their own dreams and hopes for their students. PTHVP staff often say in their trainings that this one exchange is the most important part of the visit—that if a teacher went to a home, shared his/her hopes and dreams and asked the student and family (students are strongly encouraged to be part of these visits) about theirs, then it would be a successful visit. "The rest is gravy," says Rose. "This part of the conversation is where the trust-building begins and families and teachers begin to share a common vision regarding success for a particular student" (Rose in conversation with author 2008).

Finally, teachers share their expectations for the student, ask the family what expectations they might have for the teacher, learn the best ways and times they can contact the parent, and share their own contact information. An invitation can also be offered to the parent to come to a school event or visit the classroom.

At the end of the visit, teachers can ask the parent if they would be open to the teacher returning later in the school year for a follow-up visit.

SCHEDULE OF VISITS:

Typically, home visits come during two times. The first visits, which are focused on relationship-building, occur during the fall. The second ones happen in the spring. Though they, too, help build relationships, that foundation had been laid in the fall so the spring visits can also be focused on sharing practical tools and important information that can build upon student strengths and effectively address their challenges.

Not only does the relationship-bond contribute towards making this second, more challenging visit a success, but the knowledge learned in the first visit helps teachers develop a better "frame" for the conversations. For example, instead of telling the parent that their child needs to do his homework to pass the class, the teacher can say, "In our last visit you shared your hopes that John would get good grades and be able to enter a professional career. That sounded great to me then, and sounds great to me now. We just need to figure out how he can develop the self-discipline he needs to achieve that, which includes doing his homework each night." Often during these second visits teachers also provide individualized "toolkits" to parents that are designed to help the parent help their child.

These kinds of conversations do not have to wait until the second visit, however. Many teachers report that phone conversations following the first visit are often more pleasant and effective than with parents whom have not received a visit.

COORDINATION:

The PTHVP believes it is important to have one person at the school coordinating the visits. This person is responsible for helping to organize trainings, follow-up and "de-brief" teachers after the visits have been done, and to ensure that teachers are indeed paid for their time. Depending on funding availability, at some schools this responsibility is taken as a voluntary position or a staff-person is paid a small stipend.

Since 1999, the PTHVP has worked with school districts around the country, in Massachusetts, Ohio, Colorado, and Missouri, to help organize thousands of parent/teacher home visits. The state of California has been so impressed with the work that the legislature passed a law (The Nell Soto Parent/Teacher Involvement Program Grant) that provides $15 million to schools who want to have their staff make home visits. In addition, the organization has received a grant from the United States Department of Education to help other communities begin similar projects.

Richard Riley, former U.S. Secretary of Education, said this about the PTHVP: "I urge all communities to study (this project) and use it as a model for their own home visit program" <http://findarticles.com/p/articles/mi_puca/is_200005/ai_4220020674/pg_1>. The magazine *Edutopia* named PTHVP one of the ten "Big Ideas for Better Schools" in its September, 2005 edition. And Carolyn Doggett, the Executive Director of the California Teachers Association, said, "This project is one of the best in the nation" (email to the author, August 6, 2008).

Jeannie Cowan, the author of an independent evaluation of the Sacramento PTHVP, wrote that both parents and teachers feel more comfortable communicating with each other as a result of the home visits, and that parents are more involved in their child's educational process through assisting and reviewing homework. Standardized test scores also increased in the schools doing home visits at a higher rate than the Sacramento School District as a whole. In the words of the report, "Student performance has improved over the three years of the project's implementation; parental involvement has increased, and communication between home and school has been enhanced" (4). The same evaluation concluded that improved student-teacher relationships were another positive outcome of the home visits. Students said they felt more comfortable approaching teachers, and teachers:

> … overwhelming[ly] believed their attitudes toward their students had been positively influenced by their home visits; they also felt that they had "a better understanding of their students' lives and priorities." (Cowan 21)

The PTHVP recently initiated a pilot home-visiting project targeting entering eleventh-grade students who had not passed the California High School Exit Exam (CAHSEE) on their first try as tenth graders. This effort was somewhat different from its other home visits. The purpose of this new project, in addition to relationship-building, was to specifically help families gain a greater understanding of this newer graduation requirement, help school staff gain a greater understanding of the needs and challenges facing at-risk students, and to help students participate more in school efforts to prepare them for the CAHSEE. All these goals were pointing to the primary one of increasing CAHSEE pass rates and, as a result, graduation rates, for these at-risk students.

An evaluation of the Evaluation of the CAHSEE Home Visit Pilot Project, written by Paul Tuss of the Center for Student Assessment and Program Accountability, Sacramento County Office of Education, recommended expanding the project and wrote:

> The findings to date suggest that, in seeking to increase communication and improve school/home relationships and academic outcomes for at-risk

students, the CAHSEE Home Visit Pilot Project has met with success at an institutional level. At the attitudinal level, this includes increasing understanding among parents and students regarding critical school issues, and among school staff regarding the needs and challenges facing at-risk students. At the behavioral level, this includes successfully encouraging students to participate in CAHSEE prep classes. (33)

Whose Energy Drives This Project and Who Initiated It?

In the case of the Sacramento PTHVP, the impetus came from parents who were part of an organization of religious congregations and neighborhood institutions (Sacramento Area Congregations Together—ACT). They felt that communication was poor between many parents and the schools their children attended.

They viewed this issue through a classical community organizing "lens." Using that perspective, problems usually exist for one of three reasons:

1. Decision-makers and other stake holders know it exists, but do not know how to solve it. In that case, the best solution is to bring stake-holders together to develop a joint solution.

2. Decision-makers and other stake holders do not know the problem exists. In that case, they need to be first told about the problem and then brought together to develop a joint solution.

3. Decision-makers and other stake holders know it exists, but have other competing pressures (limited resources, time, etc.) that prevent them from solving the problem (and often times they don't know how to solve it, either). In that case, prior to bringing stake-holders together to develop a solution, proponents need to demonstrate there is a sufficient constituency that feels solving the problem should be a priority.

Through hundreds of individual meetings (and neighborhood house meetings) within ACT's member institutions and then with other decision-makers and stake holders, ACT was able to develop a strong alliance with the two other key institutions in the public schools—the school district and the teacher's union.

Other successful home-visiting projects across the country use a similar model of a cooperative effort between a local community organization, the local teacher's union, and the school district. Having parents as partners can solidify community support; help keep the project's focus on relationships; and assist the school, teachers, and school district—in the face of all its other daily challenges—keep the home visits as a priority.

Some schools and districts, however, do have effective home-visiting projects that they initiate on their own, such as one 3,000 student district in Kentucky that has teachers visit the family of every student once a year (Middleton 2008).

What Are the Roles of the Parents and School Staff in This Project?

Parents and teachers are partners in this kind of a home visiting effort. In fact, the PTHVP makes that very clear in what it lists as the first thing "Our Project Members Believe:"

> Parents and teachers are equally important co-educators given that the parent is the expert on the individual child while the teacher is the expert on the curriculum that must be mastered for success. <http://www.pthvp.org/history.html>

This belief is clearly communicated in a number of ways, not least being that parents, as well as teachers, lead the required three-hour home-visit trainings.

Just the actual act of visiting a home sends a similar message. Mai Xi Lee, a vice-principal at Luther Burbank High School in Sacramento, explains:

> We're a Title I school. A lot of our folks are non-English speakers. So when they come to the school it's a huge risk-taking effort … This [home visit] is on their turf, it's their comfort zone. It turns the table onto the teachers, the educators, to go in and be the outsiders. (Lee in *The Parent Home Visiting Project DVD*, 2006)

This "co-educator" perspective differs from the "deficit model" of low-income families that has gained popularity in some education circles. The deficit model tends to view families more often as part of the problem instead of being a key part of the solution in improving student achievement.

James Keddy from PICO explains that "it's a shift in how parents see themselves—not as spectators. You see yourself as an asset. An asset in your child's life; an asset in the life of your local school, and an asset in a larger community that's trying to make a difference for kids over the long term" (Keddy in *The Parent Home Visiting Project* DVD, 2006).

Jocelyn Graves, a parent and leader in the PHVP put it this way:

> At one time I looked at teachers as educated, and I'm not educated. And so it's a good feeling for us to be sitting at the same table, being

able to communicate and talk to one another without blaming one another. (Graves in *The Parent Home Visiting Project* DVD, 2006)

Nancy Fong, a second grade teacher at Earl Warren Elementary School in Sacramento, also shared her perspective:

> I have attended many professional teacher trainings on effective curriculum deliverance but nothing is better use of my time than spending 30 minutes at a home visit….It is the one thing that I point to that keeps my enthusiasm high as a veteran teacher. (email to author, April 11, 2008)

What Is the Purpose, Who Has the Decision-Making Power, and What Kinds of Partnerships Are Developed in This Project?

The primary purpose for home visits done through the PTHVP is to build relationships. It is not a needs assessment, intervention, survey, or interview. Fred Rose, an organizer with the Pioneer Valley Project in Springfield, Massachusetts, which has worked with the PTHVP to start a similar program there, says that it's important to "put the relationship-building first. If you build the relationships you can work on the academic and work on the other issues and concerns as they come up" (Rose in *The Parent Home Visiting Project* DVD, 2006). As Rose states, and as the previously cited evaluations of the project attest, "leading" with this kind of relationship-building can result in more parent engagement in schools and greater student achievement.

In addition, one of the goals of the home-visiting process is to assist parents to develop and deepen relationships with each other, and to then subsequently work together with the school and other institutions on issues of common concern. Parents at Luther Burbank High School, for example, identified a number of issues they wanted to learn more about—particularly around issues related to immigrant legal rights—and worked with the local school and a university to develop a multi-lingual "Parent Academy."

Decision-making authority for the PTHVP, and the similar organizations it works with throughout the United States, typically lies with three key stakeholders: a community organization including parents, the local teacher's union, and the school district. This kind of equal partnership provides the project with public credibility and the resources necessary to ensure that teachers are compensated for their visits.

What Are Some Potential Challenges in Starting a Project Like This?

The challenges in starting and sustaining a home visiting project usually fall into four categories: money, teacher concerns, logistical issues, and working with partners.

MONEY:

One important reason for the success of the PTHVP is that teachers are compensated for their time if they choose to voluntarily participate. This added incentive is important to help teachers make time to do the visits since many feel they already have considerable uncompensated responsibilities and work extra hours to accomplish them.

Many private foundations have supported the launch and expansion of this effort. In lower-income communities, some schools use their Title I monies (funds that are specifically provided to schools in low-income areas), to provide these stipends. The Pioneer Valley Project in Massachusetts worked with the school district to include home visit funding in a federal grant for local magnet schools. In California and in other states the teacher's associations have provided grant monies. Also in California the statewide PICO organization was successful in getting the legislature to appropriate funds to support schools that wanted to initiate a home visit program. This kind of added political support is yet another reason for schools to begin these efforts with community partners. The Ohio Children's Foundation was successful in obtaining money from Temporary Assistance For Needy Families (federal funds provided to the state by the U.S. Department of Health and Human Services) to support teachers visiting incoming kindergartners. Finally, other state and federal grants (i.e., *No Child Left Behind*) may provide additional resources to encourage parent participation in the life of their child's schools.

TEACHER CONCERNS:

 The PTHVP has found three common concerns that arise in their teacher training workshops. One is that some teachers are worried about going alone or have other safety concerns. Some suggested responses to this concern include going in pairs and teachers leaving their schedules with the school office. In the thousands of home visits made over the years through the PTHVP, no one has ever been harmed.

Another concern is what a teacher should do if he/she sees something at the home that he/she is mandated to report to a public agency. Again, in the experience of the PTHVP, this situation is extremely rare since advance notice is given for the home visits and the model used is designed for everyone involved to be respectful. However, if teachers find something that they believe requires filing a report, the organization recommends they follow the normal reporting process for their school.

A third concern from teachers is that they might accidentally offend the family's culture or traditions in the course of a visit. The PTHVP's response is first that families tend to be forgiving of these kinds of missteps since in most cultures teachers are respected. In addition, teachers could also try to learn a little more about the traditions and history of their students' families before their visit—either through talking to other school staff, using the Internet, or talking to community organizations. Many teachers ask for additional cultural competency training during the three hour home-visiting training. However, as Carrie Rose explains, "In our experience, at the end of the day, the best way to build cultural competency is to just get out there and visit with their students' families!"

LOGISTICAL ISSUES:

There are a number of logistical questions that need to be answered, including the following:

- Who can coordinate home visits on your site, and can the coordinator be compensated?

- What are district policies regarding insurance coverage for home visitors (usually they are considered an extension of the workday and covered by worker's compensation)?

- What is the site plan for choosing students to visit?

- How will translation be handled—both on the phone to arrange the visits and during the visits themselves?

WORKING WITH PARTNERS:

Carrie Rose from the PTHVP says that when people hear about their work, many are "struck by the fact that a community organization (Sacramento ACT), a school district, and a teacher's union came together to form a non profit organization (PTHVP) and have stayed together for ten years" (conversation between Rose and Ferlazzo 2008).

All the partners have integral roles in the development and ongoing operation of the program. ACT provides the home visit training to teachers, works to develop home visit best practices based on the experiences among the many schools and districts participating, and works for increased public support from the California state legislature. The school district administers the financial support to teachers and encourages schools to participate in the effort. The teacher's union provides additional financial support, assistance regarding the inclusion of home visit activities in contract language, and encourages its members to make home visits.

This long-term cooperative arrangement is certainly unusual, though other groups with whom the PTHVP has worked with throughout the country have been able to develop similar partnerships.

Though all three entities might have conflicting interests in other arenas, they have been able to keep that tension away from the home visiting program and concentrate on their common interest in ensuring its success.

Other groups across the country who have modeled their work on the Sacramento success say that, in addition to their local partners, it has been important to work with the PTHVP in beginning their efforts. Peggy Castro from the Ohio Children's Foundation, whose project has assisted in nearly 6,000 home visits so far, says:

> Without technical assistance and training from The Parent/Teacher Home Visit Project out of Sacramento, California, it's doubtful [our effort] would have enjoyed the success it has … We adopted their philosophy of home visits. The PTHVP also trained our teachers for the first three years of our initiative. (email to author, August 8, 2008)

Many teachers and parents feel the challenges of starting a home visiting program are worth confronting. As parent Jocelyn Graves says:

> I have changed a whole lot. Now I'm not afraid to ask questions about my child. At one time I would never do that. If I had never had that home visit, my son would never have walked across that [graduation] stage. (Grave in *The Parent Home Visiting Project* DVD, 2006)

CHAPTER 3

Technology and Family Literacy

Portions of this chapter originally appeared in
TechLearning Educators' eZine *and are reprinted with permission.*

THE SILKWORM AND THE SPIDER

Having received an order for twenty yards of silk from Princess Lioness, the Silkworm sat down at her loom and worked away with zeal. A Spider soon came around and asked to hire a web-room nearby. The Silkworm acceded, and the Spider commenced her task and worked so rapidly that in a short time the web was finished. "Just look at it," she said, "and see how grand and delicate it is. You cannot but acknowledge that I'm a much better worker than you. See how quickly I perform my labors." "Yes," answered the Silkworm, "but hush up, for you bother me. Your labors are designed only as base traps, and are destroyed whenever they are seen, and brushed away as useless dirt; while mine are stored away, as ornaments of Royalty."

"True art is thoughtful, delights and endures."
Aesop's Fables <http://www.pacificnet.net/~johnr/aesop/>

T he spider thought her web would be the best—it looked beautiful at first glance. But it was built for the short-run.

It is the same for schools who want to encourage parent participation. Schools, using a parent *involvement* model, might be able to quickly design a program that could very well, at first glance, look like the technology-enhanced Family Literacy Project that will be described in this chapter (or, in fact, any of the projects discussed in this book).

The danger, however, is if it is not done in the context of a less task-focused and more relationship-oriented parent *engagement* strategy, the driving energy is less likely to come from the parents and could therefore be less successful over the long-run.

This chapter will share an example of using technology to engage parents and then analyze it through the lens of the characteristics of an effective parent engagement strategy.

What Is the Background to the Family Literacy Project?

"You haven't really lived," a teacher shared with his colleagues at the end of a school day in 2005, "until you've tried teaching a group of high school age pre-literate students how to use a computer and the Internet for the first time on a day when the school's server keeps crashing!"

So went the inauspicious first day of trying to integrate technology into an unusual high school class. Two thousand Hmong refugees arrived in Sacramento in 2004/05, and many of the high school age youth in that group came to Luther Burbank High School.

The Hmong are an ethnic group from Laos that provided tens of thousands of soldiers to the C.I.A. during the Vietnam War. The U.S. Government had promised that, if they lost the war, it would bring the Hmong to the United States. Thousands had come over the years, and the last Hmong refugee camp in Thailand, housing 10,000 people, was closed in 2005. California's Central Valley and St. Paul, Minnesota have the largest concentrations of Hmong residents. Since this last resettlement program was based on family connections, many of the final refugees arrived in these same two areas. They joined the 1,200 other English Language Learners at Luther Burbank High School.

Few of the new students had ever attended school before. No one in their families had, either. It was indeed an extraordinary opportunity. How often can a high school teacher say that his/her class is the first experience of school for his/her students? Of course, with that opportunity came challenges, and teachers began to explore a variety of teaching tools and strategies to meet them.

Much of the successful teaching of English at the school is built around the concept that one of the best ways for students to become better readers is to read high-interest books of their own choosing. This approach has been called "free voluntary reading" by Stephen Krashen (Krashen 2005). However, pre-literate students do not have this option.

As students began to learn English and become acclimated to their new country, the question arose about how to implement free voluntary reading. In addition to being a key component of mainstream English classes in the school, it also certainly fit into a community organizing philosophy of assisting people to freely choose and act on their own behalf. The school didn't have a hundred tutors that could work individually with each student, so another way needed to be found.

A teacher remembered that there were free websites that had audio and animated "talking books" available online. Community organizers (and many classroom teachers) have been generally skeptical of some uses of the Internet, since the thinking is that face-to-face contact is what is really needed to engage people. However, there is also an important essay that is required reading for many community organizers entitled "The Importance of Being Unprincipled." It's a deliberately provocative title, and the point of the article is that many of us turn far too many beliefs into principles, which dictionaries define as a "fundamental truth." It's pretty difficult to compromise on fundamental truths. The essay challenges us to reconsider what we feel are our principles, and proposes that we should only have a small number of them if we want to be effective in the world.

> "Five months after the computer lab began, English Language Learners participating scored a fifty percent greater gain on reading comprehension assessments than English Language Learners who did not come to the lab."

With that perspective in mind Burbank teachers began to explore how they could take advantage of computer technology to help implement free voluntary reading with students *and* develop strategies to use the same technology to help students develop and deepen face-to-face relationships.

The school created a webpage <http://larryferlazzo.com/english.html> with links to a few of these free sites, and opened a before-and-after school computer lab for Hmong and other English Language Learner students.

Within two weeks over 100 students were coming each day. Students were provided headphones, and became able to access any of the now over 8,000 links that are specifically accessible to English Language Learners and related to all academic subjects. In addition to just engaging with the computer screen, students would discuss in class what they were reading and make recommendations to each other— plus participate in other technology activities in small groups.

How Did the Family Literacy Project Begin?

Parents and other family members had enthusiastically participated in several school events where their children demonstrated their work on the Internet. At about the same time, teachers began making home visits with an interpreter to meet the families. One of the questions asked in these visits was what challenges they were facing, and what ideas they had about meeting those challenges. Language and transportation were common concerns. Most of the refugee parents and older children could not read in any language, so were unable to obtain a driver's license. Sacramento has a limited mass transit system, and since most high school age Hmong refugees in Sacramento were sent to Burbank, many came from a distance. These challenges made it difficult for parents to attend English classes or come to Burbank to use the computer lab on a regular basis—even if there were a class for adults there.

> One parent said, "It would be great if we could get a computer and Internet like in school. We could use it to help us learn English."

Bingo! Families could read stories together on the computer and talk about them. This approach would mirror the way in which literate families help their children learn to read—through bedtime stories.

The parent who brought up the idea agreed to talk with other families about it. Coincidentally, the school was replacing all the computers in the lab and the principal agreed to provide them to families. A private foundation agreed to provide a small grant to pay for DSL service. And soon, the families of the twenty students in one class had a home computer and DSL service and acted as a pilot project.

Parents, students, and teachers developed a set of guidelines. Eighty percent of the residents of each household needed to agree to use the website a minimum of one hour each day. All family members could use it at the same time if they wanted, and that was even preferred. They kept a simple log, and they could use the computer the other twenty-three hours a day in whatever way they wanted (their home Internet service passed through the school district's content filter, so there were some limits). Students and parents all took simple English assessments before they received the computers, as did a control group.

At the end of four months, the students with home computers had almost double the improvement in English as the control group. And, even more importantly, many students and their families volunteered that one of their favorite elements of the project was being able to read the same stories and talk with each other about them afterwards. Pade Yang, a program participant, said, "My little brothers and sisters, and Mom, read with me on the computer. I help them. We learn new words and how to say them when we see them and the computer say them. I like reading together."

In addition, many also shared that they felt much more confident speaking English as a result of using the home computers. Finally, family members were also able to become producers of online content and not just consumers; they created their own storybooks that were posted on the website.

A priority of the project was to encourage families to use the computer *together*. In fact, there were a number of built-in incentives to do so, including the fact that everyone using the computer at the same time would be able to count that time towards their individual time requirement, as well as the obvious advantage of having the more advanced English learners be able to help those in the family with a lower proficiency in English. The computer project actually reinforced the importance of relationships and reminded us that it's really the face-to-face ones—the ones that will be the primary sources of support in one's life—that are most critical. Instead of just developing a relationship with the computer screen, the school wanted families to be able to see this project as a tool to help deepen their relationships with each other.

Redwood trees in California can grow quite tall on their own. But it's when they are together in groves when they can reach their truly towering heights. That's because their roots spread underground and interlock to provide the necessary support to grow so high. It's similar to the use of technology in the Family Literacy Project—people could improve their English if they used the computer on their own, but Burbank teachers believe that working together with other family members was the key to the significant gains that were made.

The Sacramento City School District was so impressed with the results that it provided funds to triple the size of the project. The work was recognized at the Grand Prize Winner of the 2007 International Reading Association Presidential Award for Reading and Technology, and a number of schools and school districts around the United States who hoped to replicate the program contacted Burbank for assistance.

Forty immigrant families then received brand-new home computers and high-speed Internet service in the expanded project. These households included sixty-five Burbank students and over one hundred-and-fifty students who attend other Sacramento schools. Over one hundred other adults are members of these families. The school performed English assessments for this expanded number and a control group and found that the students with home computers had *four times* the improvement in English literacy in comparison to the control group.

The students and their families involved in the home computer project are also encouraged to make frequent trips to both school and public libraries. In fact, a local Friends of the Library group provides an extensive and high-quality home library to families who receive the home computers and to members of the control group. Research shows a huge disparity between the number of books in the homes of low-income families as opposed to the homes of higher-income ones. For example, the average Hispanic family with limited English-proficient children has about 26 books in their home (Ramirez, Yuen, Ramey and Pasta 89-121), which is about one-fifth of the U.S. average (Purves and Elley 89-121).

Students and parents say that the "talking stories" they read on the computer get them interested in reading more about the different topics. They then can get books for their home library, or from the school or public library, that build on that initial knowledge base. The reverse is also true—family members find a book that looks interesting to them and then want to read a "talking story" about the same topic. The school librarian also regularly orders large quantities of accessible books after talking with the students about their interests.

Whose Energy Drives This Project and Who Initiated It?

A parent with a language and transportation problem originated the idea of using home computers for family literacy. The Burbank teacher's response was not to start a program for him. Instead, he asked him if he thought other families might be interested in the same thing, and if he was willing to talk to some of them. The teacher communicated clearly that he would be happy to help. Together, they made up a list of families, divided them up between the two of them with the parent taking the families he knew best. They also discussed introducing the idea to others by first having parents share if they had language and transportation concerns. It was essential that the parent felt that school staff was both very supportive and very clear that, in order to proceed, he and other parents needed to feel that it was more important to him than to the teacher. Those two same continuing elements have been critical to the long-term health of the Family Literacy Project—the parent and student energy that initiated it and continues to drive it.

This core sentiment has also manifested itself to the high degree in what could be called "civic solidarity" among the students and families. They are aware that the future of the project depends on its success, and many repeatedly say that they want more families to get these home computers and high-speed Internet service. They understand that "success" is defined by the families developing their English skills, and that the odds of obtaining future funding for the program are increased if they are serious about using the computers to learn English.

What Are the Roles of the Parents and School Staff in This Project?

Many parents are leaders in the Family Literacy Project. They, along with their children, made the decisions about how to structure the project—what were reasonable amounts of time to require participants to using the computers to learn English, what percentage of household members should be expected to use the website, and what was a respectful and effective accountability system. Not only does this result in a greater investment towards using the computers for their intended purpose, but it recognizes parents (and students) as responsible community members whose opinions and thoughts are invited, appreciated, and carry weight with a public institution—a feeling that many low-and-moderate income families don't necessarily get from many other places.

The role of the school staff was not one of primarily providing services to people. It was one of asking, listening, sharing, and building relationships. Parents were asked about their own lives, in addition to being asked about the lives of their children. Staff genuinely listened to their responses, and asked more *probing*, not *prodding*, questions. But this process wasn't one of just taking a survey, doing a needs assessment, or conducting an interview. In addition to asking, teachers shared about their lives in return. Building a genuine relationship requires reciprocity, and teachers could certainly connect their life experiences of moving to a new place, job fears, family problems, and hopes for one's children to the stories parents were sharing with them.

Not only did teachers feel this reciprocal process helped them grow personally, it put them in a position to be able to *agitate* and not *irritate* parents. Teachers were able to then ask questions and make suggestions that could lead to parents taking action on the concerns, hopes, and dreams that they had voiced: Did they know other parents who might have similar concerns? Could they contact them? What were their ideas about responding to the problem?

Staff also didn't seek to "dump" tasks on people. Teachers helped parents plan next steps, did some themselves, and touched base with parents afterwards to see how things went. Parents, and students, developed greater self-confidence as they saw they could create a first-of-a-kind high-tech family literacy project.

Of course, these roles were not always so clear-cut. School staff drifted in and out of the defined areas that were just described, especially as the program entered its third year. However, the key is not whether a school is engaging, and not involving, parents all of the time. It's not an either/or world we live in. Instead, it's a world of ambiguity. The real question is: Which of the two sides does a school tend to lean towards?

What Is the Purpose, Who Has the Decision-Making Power, and What Kinds of Partnerships Are Developed in This Project?

The purpose of the Family Literacy Project was and is to support entire families and the communities in which they live. It is not to only provide assistance to the sixty-five Luther Burbank students who live in the households who have computers. There are over one-hundred-and-fifty other younger students who live there, too, and who, if they continue to live in the same neighborhood, will eventually attend the high school—even if it might be many years down the line. The more parents become engaged in the academic life of their children, the better for the long-term academic culture for everyone in that household. The more the parents learn English, the more likely they will get better paying jobs. This better pay will allow parents to spend more on the kinds of resources discussed in the first chapter—books, trips, enrichment classes—that are more prevalent in higher-income families. And the fact that parents were more engaged with their children academically may very well make it more likely that using those funds for academic resources will be a higher-priority for them.

The original plan for the project included raising funds to hire an outreach worker who would function as a community organizer. That person was going to work with the families to identify other community issues, and help them work together and help them bring others that they knew together to respond to some of those problems. However, it took a much longer time and much more energy than had originally been planned in order resolve a number of technology issues, and the school never got back to focusing on that—though the idea hasn't been completely abandoned. One of the drawbacks to being the first in the world (at least, as far as the school knows) to do something like this is you don't have the luxury of learning from others' mistakes—only your own! Anybody else starting something like this now can learn from Luther Burbank's technology trials and tribulations.

Parents and their families were key participants in all major decisions affecting the project, including the accountability system that was put in place. This system turned out well. It's doubtful that school staff could have developed one that was any better.

There is an old organizing saying: "If you don't give people the opportunity to say no, then you also don't give them the opportunity to say yes." *Real* parent (and student) participation in a parent engagement effort reflects that wisdom.

The Family Literacy Project developed two primary partnerships. One was with the Technology Department at the Sacramento City Unified School District. Their staff was, and continues to be, tremendously supportive of parent *engagement*. They have listened to what parents wanted from the inception of the project, and have always been successful in figuring out how it could be provided technologically. They have played a role the best "experts" always do—listen to what people want and use their expertise to create it, even if it's never been done before.

First, after spending days at one of the family's homes, they developed a way to have the DSL go through the school district server. Doing it that way not only provided a filter blocking inappropriate content, it also allowed the district to access certain funds to pay for the DSL service. Then, in response to the fact that the families moved quite a bit, they developed a way for everyone to be converted to wireless.

Another example of a "broad and deep" partnership is the work the school did with the Sacramento Mutual Housing Association (SMHA), a non-profit developer of resident-governed affordable housing. A number of Burbank families live in some of their units. SMHA, and some of their residents who were not participants in the Family Literacy Project, were so impressed by it that they began ESL computer labs at their projects that are structured like the after-school lab and emphasize students working with each other and not just with the computer. In addition, they have also begun providing individual home computers to some of their residents that, again, mirror how the Family Literacy Project is operated.

This type of expansion and replication serves many purposes. It provides public recognition to Burbank families—*they* become the experts, and that will only enhance self-confidence and their commitment to the program and to learning English. It provides additional academic support to many more students who are attending, or who might be attending, Burbank High School or other public schools in the Sacramento area. And it offers opportunities for more parents to be able to access higher-paying jobs in the future because of their improved English skills.

What Are Some Potential Challenges in Starting a Project Like This?

There are obviously many technical issues that can arise in a technology-related project. Most can be "pre-empted" by making sure up-to-date computers are used to avoid constant breakdowns, and by providing Internet access via a wireless card. When the project expanded beyond the pilot group with new computers and wireless cards, the number of technical problems reported by families plummeted.

Raising funds to support a Family Literacy Project like this one is another challenge. The project is supported by both the Sacramento School District itself and the high school. Once the computers are purchased, the primary cost of the program then becomes only the monthly Internet charges until the computers become obsolete. Doubling or quadrupling the rate of English improvement for well over 200 students was deemed worth spending $35,000 a year, which is roughly the cost for Internet service and technical assistance.

Hardware costs can be reduced considerably by school districts if they do not have a "sole-source" contract with one company to purchase only their computers and seek-out lower-priced models. Other sources of private grant monies can be found in the "Resources" section near the end of the book.

Finally, one of the biggest challenges is to approach a project like this as a parent *engagement* strategy, and to avoid doing it as part of parental *involvement.* On many levels it's easier and less messy to have school staff *start* a program like this without engaging parents. However, *starting* and *sustaining* the project are two decidedly different things.

To paraphrase Fred Ross, a legendary community organizer, short cuts will often take you to detours, which in turn can lead you to dead-ends.

CHAPTER 4

Parent Engagement through School-Community Gardens

THE FARMER AND HIS SONS

A father, being on the point of death, wished to be sure that his sons would give the same attention to his farm as he himself had given it. He called them to his bedside and said, "My sons, there is a great treasure hid in one of my vineyards." The sons, after his death, took their spades and mattocks and carefully dug over every portion of their land. They found no treasure, but the vines repaid their labor by an extraordinary and superabundant crop.

Aesop's Fables <http://www.pacificnet.net/~johnr/aesop/>

O ften, young people reject tradition, believing that there are more exciting treasures to be found. Yet nothing is more basic than the ability to grow food, and few funds of knowledge are more culturally universal than knowledge of horticulture. This is one of many reasons to develop school community gardens, which enable communities to display their horticultural knowledge, while providing a living laboratory where science, social studies (heritage traditions and oral history), nutrition, writing, and more can be studied. In the process of studying the many aspects of gardens that can be recorded and shared, communities can become involved in literacy experiences in ways which are non-threatening and empowering.

Every community has experience, either historic or current, about gardening and food preparation. Anthropologists call this body of knowledge *ethno-botany*, referring to a community's relationship to plants at all levels, from food to fiber to medicinal and culinary uses of plants. In a world economy changing from family farms to global industries, nearly every community is in the process of losing this important fund of knowledge. In the case of immigrants new to the U.S.A., many of whom come from subsistence agricultural backgrounds, schools often inadvertently belittle traditional knowledge about food and fiber, replacing it with literacy and technology. The result is a generation of children who eat junk food and become obese, schools that encourage children to be sedentary, and an epidemic of diseases that result from these factors.

Enabling children to get exercise and learn about healthful eating through a school community garden is important in any community. This is why Delaine Eastin, serving as California's Superintendent of Schools, mandated a "garden in every school," and why this mandate has continued beyond her tenure. In urban minority communities recently displaced from an agricultural way of life, and especially in communities with little tradition of schooling, the possibility of drawing parents into engagement with schools through establishing community gardens on school sites is powerful and can build bridges with otherwise unreachable communities. This chapter describes how immigrant communities from Southeast Asia (Mien, Hmong, and Cambodians), Mexico, and Central Asia became engaged in school community gardens in West Sacramento, California. Its purpose is to show that while school gardens are a way to engage nearly any community, they can be a particularly important tool in working with immigrant communities eager to preserve and pass on their traditions to their children. In addition, when language teachers and librarians become involved in chronicling these traditions with parents and children, the result can be not only a rich garden project but also a unique kind of family literacy project.

Who Are the Mien People?

Long, long ago there were a young man and a young woman who were sister and brother. A great flood came, and they climbed up to the highest lands. After the floods, they could find no one else alive. In a panic, they asked the bamboo, the oldest and wisest plant, where they could look for the other people. The bamboo said that they were the only survivors, and that they must procreate...

When the woman had a baby, it was not a human, but a squash with many seeds. The woman sent the man out to plant the seeds all over the earth, especially in the lowlands, where they would grow well, but he tripped and became confused, and most of the seeds fell in the highlands. That is why there is only a small tribe of Mien up in the highlands, and other tribes of people inhabit the rest of the earth. (from a Mien creation story as told by parents at the Family English Literacy Project, West Sacramento, 1997)

The relationship between Mien people and their plants is without parallel in western experience, and is a key to understanding the culture of this Southeast Asian hill tribe. Mien people come from subsistence agricultural roots and from an independent, rural life-style that was tragically interrupted by the war in Vietnam. Mien people, along with their Hmong counterparts, assisted the CIA in the Secret War in Laos and had to flee their country when the Communists took over. Refugee groups of Mien were invited to the U.S.A. because of their alliance during the war. They have settled in a few areas of the United States, where they re-congregate as a tribe, and like the Hmong described in Chapter 3, many have settled in the Central Valley of California.

As a displaced agricultural people who often find themselves in urban settings, living in apartments they can afford, often near freeways and far from the rivers and mountains they once knew, these people pine for land, greenery, and collective spaces in which to gather. At a practical level, they seek places in which they can once again produce at least some of their beloved traditional foods. While part of what the Mien people seek in gardens is high quality food, it is important to understand that the plants in these gardens are more than food to them. To this day, a Mien person in trouble will seek the advice of the wise bamboo, using the shaman as a medium for doing so. From a Mien perspective, bamboo has a longer history than human beings, and unlike humans, is a producer rather than a consumer. These are things which Mien people understand deeply. To spend time with plants is to spend time in a wise and peaceful place, and to do so in community, in a shared garden, is like going back to the mountains of Asia, which are so deeply missed.

Teachers who were gardeners themselves were happy to meet the Mien and Hmong people who came to the schools where they worked, because they could understand their connection to nature and its importance to them. What, you may ask, do gardens and journeys have to do with work in an urban school?

Parent engagement in a school must be based on an understanding of the needs, priorities, and funds of knowledge of the families and communities involved in that school. In short, to work successfully with families, it is necessary to begin by understanding their cultural priorities. The garden project is not really about gardens per se. It is about the process of negotiating a meaningful space between a school and its community so that the relationships which emerge in that space develop in a manner which is authentic, productive, and sustaining. Gardens would not be the right bridge for all communities, so this chapter is about gardens as one example of an authentic school-community relationship.

In the case of the Southeast Asian community, as well as the Mexican community at other school sites, the garden provided common ground, literally and philosophically, to groups who had little or no experience with literacy, formal math, or many of the other activities which go on in schools. A partnership between parents, educators, and social agencies in the community created a series of school-community gardens as inter-cultural spaces which bridged the gap between these communities and their schools. While these gardens met true community development needs as both sources of food security (parents grew food there for use at home) and community gathering places, their purposes from the perspective of this chapter were 1) to create negotiated inter-cultural spaces which had meaning to both teachers and community members and which provided a bridge between them, and 2) to encourage literacy through the chronicling of community horticultural and culinary knowledge. Because the gardens provided a context in which knowledge could be shared and recorded through oral history projects, engagement with literacy occurred in communities not previously engaged with academic work. Many types of relationships with immigrant communities developed over a fifteen year period. The stories told are snapshots from the numerous projects that evolved over this time period, chosen from a larger photo album as an illustration of how school community gardens can provide a rich environment for parent engagement.

It is important to note that all of the projects had an effect on student achievement through the medium of increasing academic parent engagement for immigrant communities in the schools involved. Research (Epstein 701-712) shows that parent engagement increases students' academic achievement, and that the effect is greater when parents are involved in academic rather than purely social pursuits. The garden projects provided a way for non-literate parents to participate in meaningful literacy events through the recording of their horticultural and culinary knowledge, and to see their knowledge valued. This tied them both to literacy and to the school as an institution which valued their traditions, which in turn led to increased parent engagement with other school events and increased achievement by their children.

Story #1: Creating the Evergreen School Community Garden

The staff of a Family English Literacy Project (FELP) in a low income apartment complex occupied by Mien and other Southeast Asian refugee families initiated the idea of starting a school science garden at Evergreen School, a neighborhood elementary school which their children attended in West Sacramento. At the first meeting, about twenty-four parents, mostly Mien, were gathered in one of the apartment living rooms, which had been furnished with tables and chairs and converted into a cramped classroom. The parents had notebooks, for practicing taking notes in English. Many of the women had babies tied on their backs, but older children were playing in a bedroom, which had been converted into a small daycare center. A translator was present.

The teachers began the meeting by asking parents whether gardens were important to them. Parents were eager to move on to more practical questions. They answered quickly that in Laos and Thailand, gardens had been the most important thing in their lives, since they were their source of food. This seemed obvious to them. They wanted to know if the project could help them to get land for gardening. At another school, with Hmong and Cambodian parents, teachers had recently had the same conversation, but parents had been even more blunt. "We don't do meetings," one parent said, "we do gardens." The teachers had wanted to see a big turn-out at a meeting, to show that there was enough interest to do the garden. But few parents attended school meetings. On the garden day, however, the staff was amazed when eighty family members showed up with hoes over their shoulders, and dug up the whole garden in one day.

The district-wide bilingual science coordinator and the coordinator of a multicultural library were hired to create meaningful, community-based science projects in the district's urban schools. The task of these two district level staff people was in part to link the parents' self interest in having a garden to grow their own food to the school's interest in gardens as 1) demonstrations of traditional horticulture, 2) places where children could grow crops, and 3) locations for parent engagement with the school. The district coordinators had already met with teachers, administrators, and librarians at Evergreen School who wanted a school garden for science and social studies projects. Evergreen teachers were concerned that they did not have the energy to maintain a garden in addition to doing their classroom work. They hoped that parents would help, especially during school vacations. They also hoped that a garden would help them make contact with refugee parents with whom they had trouble communicating, because of a lack of common language and cultural differences. The coordinators' job was to negotiate between their concerns and those of the immigrant parents.

The coordinators asked the parents if in exchange for a family garden plot, they would be willing to help maintain a school garden plot, and to work with teachers on gardening lessons. The Mien parents talked among themselves, then expressed concern through the translator about communicating with the teachers. They said that they would be willing to go as a group, but not to go alone to meet with a class. They agreed that they would be willing as a group to maintain the school plots during vacations, taking turns watering and weeding. It became clear that the coordinators also needed someone with whom teachers could communicate, to organize the group. The Family Literacy Director knew that the shaman's family was central in organizing this Mien community. She asked who would like to serve as a link to the parents, and was pleased when the star English student and the shaman's daughter-in-law volunteered to be a garden coordinator.

Several district coordinators and the FELP director soon began to work with the immigrant garden coordinator and her extended family to organize the creation of a garden at Evergreen School. They found that they could rely on her to bring Mien parents to the school when they were needed to do a garden day, to distribute garden plots fairly among the Mien community (families competed over plots, which were extremely valuable to them), and to transmit rules for garden use (such as water protocols and prohibitions on the use of pesticides). This same woman served as the garden coordinator at Evergreen School for the next twelve years, at times as a paid position (through grants received) and at times as a volunteer.

The district coordinators spent several months of negotiating with school and city officials to get a plot of land (an old baseball field), to get water, and to have the garden fenced. The land was part of a system of parks adjacent to school properties in this school district, and was jointly owned by the schools and the city. These agencies were willing to see some fields dedicated to gardens after a food security grant was received from the United States Department of Agriculture (USDA), which paid for irrigation systems and fencing.

When the staff arrived at Evergreen School for the first meeting, the classroom was already crowded. Hoes in hand, and babies on backs, Mien families, including mothers, fathers, and grandparents were ready to work. A handful of Central Asian and white parents were present too. The big subject of interest was the allocation of plots. A plot plan which had been drawn and laid out with sticks and string by the Mien garden coordinator, her husband, and some school staff members was shown to the parents. They were told that in the morning, they would be digging the twenty plots marked for the school classrooms. Then at lunch, they would receive their family plots. Parents were also given keys to the garden, an action which had been painstakingly negotiated with school district officials. The question was whether parents being on school grounds (but not able to enter the school) on evenings and weekends would create a threat of vandalism. It was hard for school officials to relinquish control of the keys to community people, yet at all five school gardens the schools experienced a decrease in vandalism when parents were there on weekends and, in effect, patrolled the school site.

By 9:30 AM, everyone poured out of the room toward the garden, which was at this point an irregularly shaped half-acre of weeds. One teacher carried several digging spades which she had purchased at a hardware store. An older Mien woman, carrying her hand-forged sharpened hoe, felt the bottom of the teacher's dull shovels and said "bad tools." This was the first of many experiences the staff would have working with a more knowledgeable community of gardeners.

The morning was one of those clear, spring days after a rain, when the valley air has become soft and warm for the first time. Many women were dressed in brightly colored cotton wrap-around skirts. Barefoot or in slip-on sandals, they hoed together in rows of two or three, rapidly clearing sod, digging up the ground underneath, and burying the layer of sod about ten inches under the ground, so that it would break down and fertilize the soil, but not re-sprout as weeds (as was explained in a later interview). Many mothers hoed with babies on their backs, tied in brightly embroidered carriers. Toddlers and preschoolers took small hoes that had been bought for the school children and attempted to dig. From time to time, families sat under a tree at the edge of the garden for a few minutes, unpacked sticky rice and some kind of condiment, and shared a snack.

There was a dream-like quality to the day. The schoolyard had been transformed into a tribal community at work. People called to each other in Mien as they worked, laughing and joking. No one yelled at a child, nor did any children fight. It was apparent that this group had worked together for a long time. By noon, all of the school plots were transformed from a field covered in high grass to neatly dug mounds, ready to plant. After lunch, parents received their family plots. A teacher went by the school to pick up tools at 5:00 PM, and found that families were still there, schoolage children having joined their younger siblings, and everyone was still at work. By the next week, there were green sprouts all over the field, and by midsummer, it had become a field of corn and other vegetables, all immaculately tended: a museum of traditional horticulture for the school to study and enjoy.

Story #2: Community-Based Science and Nutrition: The Mustard Greens Festival

> *Mustard greens saved our lives many times in Asia, because they grow when other crops fail. This is why we must give thanks to them by teaching our children to grow and eat them.* (A Mien grandmother on the Harvest Greens Festival Day, 2001)

Traditional approaches to parent "involvement" ask parents to participate in the business of the school in ways that may not match the skills or needs of diverse, urban parents. At Evergreen School, most parents work long hours and are not free to come to school to assist in classrooms. In the Mien and other immigrant communities, however, grandparents are often free during the day. These caregivers, who pick up the children from school on foot, do not speak English and often have never attended school themselves. Most are illiterate, in English or in any other language. Teachers have not historically involved immigrant extended families in school activities, since they do not speak English and are unfamiliar with school tasks such as photocopying, helping children with reading or math, or selling cupcakes at a bake sale.

With the garden came new opportunities for parent engagement for school staff members who were open to changing their views. Grandparents began spontaneously to share vegetables with teachers when they picked up their grandchildren from school. An after-school science project began to organize garden days when grandparents would help children to plant in their garden plots. On one occasion, two Mien grandparents brought a propane stove which they set up in the garden and cooked a stir fry of vegetables for children to taste. From these activities, the concept of school-wide garden and nutrition days was created based on the harvest of crops which the families had in abundance at certain times of the year. The Mustard Green Festival was one such occasion.

Mustard greens are grown in every Mien garden during the fall-spring winter gardening season. They grow abundantly even in cold weather, and when complimented with cilantro, green onions, and snow peas, they can be relied on to provide high vitamin greens all winter long. In the spring, the garden plots overflow with greens, which soon go to seed. Families have plenty to share with the school community.

As part of the garden project, the partnership of coordinators, community workers and teachers who had now formed around the garden project wrote for and received a food security grant from the Department of Agriculture. The purpose of this grant was to help fund the school garden projects and to create a link between the gardens and the school lunch program. Mien parents at Evergreen and Mexican parents at another garden school had the opportunity to train to be cafeteria workers, under the tutelage of the school district food director. They were able to build on their traditional knowledge of cooking to learn the skills of a professional cook. Their job was to cook monthly ethnic lunches in the cafeteria, based on food from the school garden. This enabled diverse schoolchildren to celebrate the ethnic foods eaten by some of their peers, and increased the nutritional qualities of the school lunches by adding fresh vegetables. When it came time to cook mustard greens, the garden committee consisting of the Mien garden coordinator, several teachers, and the district partners were concerned about whether or not the schoolchildren would eat mustard greens. The group decided to have a "Mustard Greens Festival" involving the whole school community, as a kind of marketing device the day of the mustard green lunch.

Mien gardeners assembled, along with interested teachers, to plan this day. The teachers and district coordinators came up with science lessons on the life cycle of mustard, which could be viewed in all stages in different parts of the garden. Sixth graders were trained in spotting mustard in its different forms, and took small groups of younger children on garden tours searching for mustard sprouts, flowers, etc. Teachers created a poster of the four stages in the plant's life cycle, which was later amended by the elders who wanted to add two stages, in order to capture more nuances related to the cooking of mustard greens (young leaves are cooked a different way than more mature leaves, for example). Then the elders came up with the idea of each child planting a mustard seed in a cup, to grow in the classroom or take home. The seeds were ones they had saved from their own mustard plants. It was their desire to spread mustard plants everywhere, based upon their gratefulness at how mustard plants had saved their lives in Asia. Each grandmother carefully extracted a bundle of seeds from her collection, which would support her own planting of mustard the next season, and gave them to the schoolchildren, who carefully planted a seed in a paper cup. The lesson on life cycles could hardly have been clearer.

When mustard greens from the garden were served stir fried with ground pork and spices in the school cafeteria that day, the dish sold out before the teachers could even deliver a plate to the superintendent. Since urban children too often eat "junk food," even in school cafeterias, it was gratifying to see them wolfing down their mustard greens and rice.

Story #3: Building a Mien-American House

One day several Mien people were talking about how in Laos, the fields are in the mountains at some distance from their villages, so every field has a small "field house" which serves as a place to rest, cook a meal, or even spend the night. They began to think how nice it would be if a field house could be built in the Mien school garden, as a place to rest and a reminder of past lives in Laos. This possibility was discussed with the teachers, who came up with the idea that a small house could serve as a storytelling place, where elders or teachers could share stories for an audience of about 20 children. A collaboration was developing between the district bilingual science project and multicultural library, the Family Literacy Project, and an International Studies Project at a local university. The idea of holding the International Studies summer institute at Evergreen School, so that regional teachers could invent curricula related to the garden and nutrition project, generated the notion of building the Mien field house during the institute, so that visitor teachers, Mien parents, and children could work together to build the house in a traditional way.

It is important to note that various players needed to be linked for a project like this to work. An architect was hired for a small fee from the science grant to work with the staff and with Mien elders to design a field house that was like a playground structure, and did not need a building permit, and that would be safe for the children to use. The school had hired two young Southeast Asian teachers, one Hmong, one Mien, who could explain to the elders and parents involved in the project what the needs of the school would be. At every step of the way, there were inter-cultural crises. One of many examples involved the use of cement. After participants went into the countryside to cut saplings for the poles that frame the house, the architect said that it would be necessary to cement the poles in the ground instead of simply to dig them in. This angered the elders, who said that they had never used cement in Asia but their houses did not fall down. In payment for this compromise, the staff was told that they would have to provide a meal for the elders, but people feared that they would not know how to cook a proper meal. It was agreed that everyone needed to eat a peacemaking noodle lunch at the local Lao restaurant.

After many other crises, but many wonderful days of building with teachers and parents, the Mien house was complete. It was a compromise all the way. It had a Mien design, with a sleeping platform, bamboo shelves, and a fire pit. But it had cement, a tin rather than a palm roof, and nails rather than tied vines connecting it. At times, the elders upset everyone by complaining that they had been told that they were "experts," but then had their expertise challenged when the American architect required things they would not traditionally do. When the architect asked for handicapped access, one elder said: "Now we are stopping having a Mien house." In Mien culture, he explained, handicapped access is not needed because people take care of each other, and would carry a handicapped person into a building. Learning to care for each other is a part of Mien culture.

One day a shaman, the elder on the building team, hung a sacred object against the wall of the house. It consisted of a special rock on a string with pieces of paper inscribed with Chinese writing tied at intervals along the string. He showed this object to the building team, then took them over to show something else he had done, which was to use the leftover bag of cement to make a floor for the bamboo shelves. The teachers were amazed, since it was he who had objected to the cement for the posts. When he showed them, he smiled, and said "cement, good" and everyone laughed. Later that day, as the team looked from the doorway of the house at the verdant garden outside, a Mien teacher friend mused that what had been built was not a Mien house, but rather a "Mien-American house," which matched the lives of the Mien community here. Such a house is built on compromise.

Story #4: Project Cultures: Ethno-botany as Family Literacy and Science in a Mexican School Garden

One important aspect of the community garden projects at all five schools is the way in which they began to evolve in their own directions, depending on the will of the community. This is one of the ways in which the staff involved knew that the families were indeed guiding the project. While the Mien-American house at Evergreen School was being built, a Mexican garden was taking form at Westfield school.

Several Mexican teachers came up with the idea of developing an ethno-botany project focused on the uses of plants in the Mexican community as a part of the school writing project. Being a bilingual school, Westfield was under pressure to improve the literacy and writing skills of the children. However, being an 80% Latino school, many staff members were aware that both children and community got more involved when projects had a cultural aspect. The CULTURES project, funded by a Toyota Tapestry Grant, involved a partnership between Westfield School, its parent community, California State University at Sacramento and the student teachers there, and UC Davis, as represented by an ethno-botanist. The project involved students doing an oral history of their families' uses of plants for culinary and medicinal purposes, and then writing about these uses in a variety of ways including essays, stories, recipes, and more. All of this material was compiled by the community into a book and huge PowerPoint presentation. Given the right librarian working with teachers, the material could also have been transformed into a blog or website, a Wiki, board games, or any number of media products. Simultaneously, parents grew several traditional plots in the school community garden, including a *milpa* (corn, beans, and squash), and a salsa garden, so that children could witness and participate in the growing and processing of traditional crops. In addition, children learned botanical science from student teachers and the ethno-botanist. At the end of the year, several hundred family members attended a harvest dinner and PowerPoint presentation, displaying a level of parent engagement the school had never known.

What Do We Learn from These Stories from the Field?

Each of these stories from the school-community garden projects demonstrate key elements of parent engagement, as will be described below.

Who Initiates and Drives the Project?

The school community garden projects emerged from a deep interest in gardens on the part of both the Mexican and Southeast Asian communities, and a lesser interest by individuals from other communities, at five urban elementary and middle schools. The "mother" of these five gardens was a spontaneous community garden which had been started by the Southeast Asian community a few years before, on some abandoned land by the river, near the middle school. Project coordinators and teachers knew about this garden, and knew about the fact that both Southeast Asian and Mexican families in this community had been displaced from rural lifestyles in which they grew their own food. They also knew that people from these communities went to lengths to get traditional foods from a variety of markets, and that these markets did not exist in West Sacramento, where they lived. In addition, they knew that most immigrant families lived in apartments, and had no land to garden except in community plots. All of these factors worked together to create an interest and need for gardens on the part of these communities.

Being aware that the energy for the gardens could not come from the school staff, teachers and district coordinators came up with the idea of leveraging the community's interest in getting garden land to create parent engagement by requiring that families who took garden plots help maintain the student garden plots and assist the teachers in gardening instruction.

Two things are worth noting at this point. The first is that gardening is but one example of an activity which can motivate a community. Even within West Sacramento schools, there were communities of parents who were not motivated by school gardens, but who might be motivated by something else. For example, the Slavic immigrant community there, which is very large, experienced gardens in Russia when there were shortages, but was basically made up of urban people who would rather go to the supermarket than garden. However, this community was very motivated by the prospect of having a music program at the school, and contains many individuals who play instruments and are willing to teach music. The point is not so much to create a garden, as to find the activity and body of knowledge which motivates a particular community to action.

Gardens are not universally motivating, but gardens are important to a variety of different communities for different reasons. The "garden in every school" movement in California exists for several compelling reasons:

1. the high incidence of childhood obesity and of children experiencing poor nutrition, even at times due to food sold at schools;

2. the motivating and relaxing nature of gardening for children, and the fact that many things, such as science or art, can be learned in a garden;

3. the fact that many urban children are said to have "nature deficit disorder" due to their lack of experience in the natural world, and their need to appreciate and understand this world; and

4. the need to motivate under-achieving populations academically through creating a stronger connection between schools and their communities.

While not all communities share the drive to develop gardens for home use that the Mien, Hmong, and Mexican communities demonstrated in West Sacramento, many communities are willing to volunteer in school gardens and, like the immigrant communities, respond to the opportunity to contribute skills that are practical and non-academic within the school community. So many types of activities can happen in a garden, from cooking to watercolor painting to the construction of bird houses, that the proper motivational formula might be found in almost any community. There is no question that the level of interest expressed by the Southeast Asian community is specific and perhaps rare, and that each school must find the activity that motivates its particular population.

While parents were naturally motivated to develop the school gardens, it was apparent that each garden community needed to be organized by an insider to the school who knew how the school worked but who also spoke the community language and could communicate well with parents. At each school site, the staff identified such a person or persons, and when there were grants which provided garden funding, the grant-writers wrote in money to pay this person as a garden coordinator. Community members showed interest in being the garden coordinator at each site. Immigrant parents, the school custodian, language development specialists, and outreach workers were among those who became involved. This leads us to a discussion of roles.

What Is the Role of Parents in the Project?

This is a very important question. One of the project goals was to find ways to celebrate and express community "funds of knowledge" within diverse, immigrant schools, as a major focus of parent engagement activities. This commitment was based on the work of Luis Moll, Norma Gonzales, and others (Moll et al, 132-141), which discusses how middle class communities draw on parent strengths without anyone even being aware that this is happening, but low income and working class communities are often less successful at involving parents as providers rather than consumers of knowledge. Teachers and other school officials too often assume that less educated communities will have a difficult time getting involved in the educational process. However, Moll and Gonzales point out that every community has its own funds of knowledge, which it is the job of the school to figure out. Moll and Gonzales describe how they send researchers and teachers on home visits in their community to find out what parents and others in minority communities are doing, and to bring their expertise into the school curriculum. As one example, they discuss a border town where Mexican families are involved in making and importing Mexican candies, produced from fruits and other fresh ingredients. This candy-making activity was used as the basis for an exciting social studies and science unit on how to make and market candies.

In West Sacramento, the gardens provided an almost limitless set of opportunities for enriching and expanding the curriculum of the schools. Parents worked with district bilingual coordinators and multi-cultural librarians, with university partners including student teachers, and with English as a Second Language teachers to produce "big books" and little books on a variety of topics related to Mien gardens, such as books on growing rice, books on life in the village, and folk tales related to crops. Since the immigrant families there had been agricultural people, most of their stories related to the garden. At Westfield School, the ethno-botany project was also one of many in which "community books" were created by family members and placed in the school library. Through these books, students could learn about their own heritage and that of others, and they and their families could participate in creating as well as receiving knowledge.

The garden projects also sponsored a variety of family literacy activities including science nights in the garden, family math nights, and the like. The concept behind all of these is that parents can get involved in their children's educations not simply by reinforcing information from the school, but by teaching their own traditions to their children. On several occasions, the school library was used as a museum, in which children created models of their villages and crops, and the public came to see them. These projects always involved the families as sources of information.

> " The concept behind all of these is that parents can get involved in their children's educations not simply by reinforcing information from the school, but by teaching their own traditions to their children. On several occasions, the school library was used as a museum, in which children created models of their villages and crops, and the public came to see them. "

Perhaps most importantly, the project emphasized parents as expert teachers in the classroom and garden. Mien and other parents were invited to tell stories in the storytelling field house in the garden. When a summer institute was held for regional teachers, parents from all communities were invited to come to it for a week and teach summer school with the teachers, in a curriculum based on community funds of knowledge. During this week, one ethnic group made lunch each day in the school cafeteria for the whole school.

Community funds of knowledge are a kind of social capital that is often overlooked. Too often minority students are described by what they lack rather than what they have. We refer to a person as a "limited English speaker" instead of as a "Hmong speaker" or a "bilingual student," even though many immigrant children and families speak several languages prior to English. Similarly, school knowledge is often thought of as being limited to what is found in published books. **If topics of study are envisioned as an exchange between mainstream sources of knowledge and community sources of knowledge, then the knowledge which parents have takes on new value.** In the school community garden project, parents were able to take an active role in schools, as expert teachers of what they know, rather than to take a passive role as recipients of information provided by the school. The garden project provided a multitude of opportunities for knowledge exchange, since parents often had much more knowledge of gardening than did the school staff. Research on parent engagement and student achievement shows that student achievement is forwarded when parents engage in academic, rather than simply social activities at their children's schools (Epstein, 701-712). In addition, children's academic achievement goes up in proportion to increases in their parents' education. Family literacy activities engage parents not only in helping their children, but in practicing reading and writing English themselves, thus increasing their ability to help their children succeed in school.

What Is the Role of the Teacher, the Outreach Worker, or the Librarian?

One of the challenges facing any parent engagement project, including a school garden, is coordination of activities among the parties involved. Every school has a culture which involves complex structures and negotiations with which outsiders are generally not familiar. When families are unfamiliar with English and/or American culture, the situation is even more difficult. In order to engage parents in activities which interface with the school, somebody on the school staff needs to broker each situation as it arises to make sure that what "works" in the community will "work" in the school. Having a garden coordinator who is a member of an ethnic community is very helpful, but that person needs to be guided by a teacher, outreach worker, or librarian as s/he attempts to set up events and solve problems which arise. Gardens involve a variety of physical as well as human challenges. What to do when the water goes off? When the gate breaks? A teacher or teachers, or ideally a committee of people in different roles in the school, need to help oversee a garden project and to interface with the parents engaged in it. A school librarian is an ideal person to get involved because:

1. her job is often more flexible than teachers in terms of time,

2. the library is a good central clearing house and place for meetings,

3. information about gardening and garden curricula can be gotten and stored in the library, and

4. ideally, a librarian might want to engage parents and children in the making of garden books, and in the subsequent sharing of them.

What Is the Role of the Administrator(s)?

It is common for schools to say that they want parent engagement but to inadvertently make this engagement difficult. It is extremely important that schools have friendly office staffs who, despite their many obligations, are not too busy to deal with community members. School schedules are often rigid, due to organizational pressures, so that students have no time to work in the garden, or even to walk there to do other academic activities which could happen in the garden, such as reading, writing, or drawing. Rigid schedules do not encourage parent engagement, since being involved with parents takes up teachers' time, and parents often do things on their own schedules rather than on an exact school schedule. For example, it is important that if parents cook traditional foods in classrooms, staff members and administrators make time for these foods to be appreciated, even if the normal school routine is interrupted.

It is essential that principals and other administrators who want parent engagement think through how accessible their institution is to outsiders, and especially to minority parents, who might behave in different ways than expected. An administrator who is successful at working with parents will find ways to bend to their needs without disrupting the school plan, and will encourage their teachers to be flexible in their dealings with parents.

In many schools, language is a big deterrent to parent engagement. Making translators available for parents who want to participate in or make a presentation to a class is essential if language minority parents are to be involved. Welcoming younger siblings is another factor that can make it possible for parents to participate. The garden is an environment in which flexible situations, such as the presence of younger siblings, can often be more easily tolerated than in a classroom.

What Is the Purpose and Who Has the Decision-Making Power?

This is a very important question, which is closely related to the purpose of parent engagement in the first place. In a traditional parent involvement model, parents are often seen as helpers who do tasks that teachers do not have time to do. When parents do not speak English, or have little schooling themselves, or are in any other way different from teacher expectations, it can be a challenge to teachers, in that getting parents' "help" might take a significant energy output on the teachers' part. Yet since engaging parents will have profound long term gains for their students, many teachers realize that it is worth the effort. School librarians and other support staff members, who often have more flexible schedules than teachers, can also play a role in accommodating parents' needs, thus making engagement in classrooms more possible.

The main purpose of engaging parents in a school is to build social capital so that the families and through them the entire community becomes more self sufficient, more engaged in civic life, and more successful in the long run. Children reared in a community where adults are self sufficient, engaged, and successful will have these traits themselves. If parents are disenfranchised from, intimidated by, or rebellious toward school, school staff will have a very hard time overcoming these factors and helping students to succeed. Hence, it is important that schools educate parents as well as children. That is why family literacy projects are so essential. The children of parents who are educated will become educated themselves. Building strong schools is a long term proposition that involves the entire community

> " Building strong schools is a long term proposition that involves the entire community. "

In the school community garden projects in West Sacramento, decisions about each garden were made at each site, by parents and the community in conjunction with involved staff members. Each garden therefore became a reflection of its community. As has been mentioned, the Mien garden built a storytelling field house, where people gathered, napped babies, and rested out of the sun. Yet the rest of the garden was all put into crops, because growing many vegetables was a high priority to this community. In contrast, the Mexican garden at Westfield School was organized as a plaza, with a large lawn and rose bushes in the center, because that community liked to use its garden for community events. The individual nature of each garden gave each community power to develop its own values in the public space and to develop their school as a place for their community.

Communities are not just empty vessels waiting to be educated. By definition, communities have their own strengths, cultures, and languages. In some cases, these are the same as those of the school, and parent engagement is not hard to achieve. In some cases, these are different from those of the school. In these cases, it is part of the job of the school to figure out the strengths, cultures, and languages of the community, and to invite these into the school as part of the instructional plan. If school can become an exchange between community cultures and knowledge and those of the mainstream, then exciting educational opportunities can happen for teachers and students alike. There are many ways to celebrate community knowledge in a school. One of them is to create environments, such as a school-community garden, where people naturally do real and productive work, and to build interactions within that space. A school community garden which allows families to gather in it and to organize it as they like becomes a laboratory for understanding the surrounding community, and for bringing the energies of this community into the school like a bountiful harvest.

What Challenges Do School-Community Gardens Face?

Gardens require constant maintenance. School staff have enough responsibilities without becoming gardeners, and schools rarely have extra funds to pay for maintenance of gardens. While partnerships are essential to all kinds of projects, an ongoing garden is a physical proof of whether or not partnerships with parents and volunteer groups are working. A well pruned garden demonstrates care, not only of plants, but of the community itself.

What Kinds of Partnerships Are Developed?

Gardens are a long-term project which can only work if based upon broad and deep partnerships with a variety of parties. The West Sacramento school-community garden projects, which maintained large gardens at five school sites over periods ranging from two to fifteen years, involved the support and engagement of a variety of agencies at several levels. The projects were framed by a professional development school partnership with two universities, which made it possible to mobilize student teachers as people-power to work with students in the gardens through service learning projects, and to justify time on the part of faculty members who provided in-service training for teachers and staff members in science, gardening, and literacy development. It was also supported by Delaine Eastin herself, then Superintendent of California Schools, and others on her staff, who wrote support letters which helped win federal grants as well as grants from private foundations. The gardens were also linked to various curricular areas within the schools, such as science, bilingual education, family literacy, and more.

This project also partnered with a local community development agency, Project FISH, Families in Self Help, which served as the job trainer for the garden coordinators and the food service parents in training, and with a local hospital, who served as the fiscal agent for the grant from USDA. The project also partnered with the county science coordinator and her staff, who gave special events and did in-service training of teachers in science and gardening; and with an environmental institute at the local agricultural university, which provided support in the form of scientists in the schools and students who ran after-school garden clubs.

All of these partnerships are in addition to the obvious and central partnership which was developed with the family communities at each school site. Since these represented ethnic communities, they were organized in part through existing groups within each community, such as the Catholic Church, for the Mexican community, and the Mien and Hmong tribal elders.

While the circumstances in West Sacramento were unique, all communities have social capital which can be organized for the benefit of all. In poor or minority communities, this social capital includes not only the families involved, but also the institutions which work with and serve these families, and sometimes institutions such as universities which work with schools. For example, teacher education partnerships serve schools by providing people-power in the form of student teachers and other volunteers, while simultaneously providing universities with authentic settings in which to train teachers to work with diverse communities. A well organized school with special projects such as a school-community garden is easy for partners, as well as grantors, to engage with successfully. The key is to assure that partners, be they parents or institutions, feel engaged as active, powerful agents in forwarding a project which, like a well tended garden, makes everybody proud.

CHAPTER 5

Schools and Community Organizing

THE BUNDLE OF STICKS

An old man on the point of death summoned his sons around him to give them some parting advice. He ordered his servants to bring in a faggot [a bundle] of sticks, and said to his eldest son: "Break it." The son strained and strained, but with all his efforts was unable to break the bundle. The other sons also tried, but none of them was successful. "Untie the faggots," said the father, "and each of you take a stick." When they had done so, he called out to them: "Now, break," and each stick was easily broken. "You see my meaning," said their father.

"Union gives strength."
Aesop's Fables <http://www.pacificnet.net/~johnr/aesop/>

I ndividually, the sticks were weak and easily broken. However, when they were joined together their unity made them stronger.

As was discussed in the first chapter, many of the challenges that face our schools are caused by situations beyond the classroom door. This explanation is not offered as a reason for teachers, administrators, and school districts to not make positive changes within the schools on their own. Instead, it recognizes a reality that could encourage schools to work with parents and consider looking at other institutions in their broader community—religious congregations, neighborhood groups, business associations, sports clubs, etc.—as allies in combating those challenges. These same institutions can also be partners in effectively engaging parents since many parents (and students), too, participate in them. Community organizing offers, among other benefits, an avenue for schools to further encourage student success by "leveraging" the relationships parents and students already have with other institutions.

Alone, schools might not have enough power and resources to assist parents to get high-paying jobs so they can buy more books for home and support enrichment activities for their children. Alone, schools might not have enough power to ensure that parents and their children have adequate health care and have fewer absences because of less illness. Alone, schools and parents might not have enough power to make sure that local drug houses are closed down, or dangerous intersections are provided with traffic lights, so that students can walk to and from school without fear.

However, schools and parents might be able to join together with other local "mediating institutions"—groups that, like schools, have historically "mediated" between families and the cultural and economic pressures that challenge families. These partnerships could help develop the power necessary to help solve some of these issues that lie outside the schoolhouse door but have a major impact on what goes on inside the classroom. This power can be used to both develop and reinforce greater community support for student success (public recognition of parents and students at religious services and neighborhood events, school-based "parent academies") and to negotiate with public and corporate officials/leaders to obtain increased resources (school health clinics, after-school programs, public safety improvements, paid on-the-job internships, business-supported scholarships, better facilities) that would enhance school and neighborhood conditions for students to learn.

There are also other potential benefits to this kind of relationship. The development of these kinds of supportive constituencies can result in additional overall support for public schools. And, in addition to gaining a better education for their neighborhood's children, numerous studies have shown that better schools can help neighborhoods realize increased local property values and reduced crime rates (The RAND Corporation, 16-18).

This chapter will look at a few examples of how schools and parents have engaged in community organizing as a way to develop these kinds of relationships. There are a number of organizations throughout the United States that are doing this kind of work with schools and parents. This section will more specifically look at the Industrial Areas Foundation (IAF), the largest community organizing network in the United States. The IAF began working with schools nearly forty years ago. Its most well-known school-related project is the Alliance Schools in the Southwest. This chapter will discuss both that project's history and its recent developments. In addition, it will talk about two other efforts in California that IAF organizer Maribeth Larkin explains "have been informed" by the work of the Alliance Schools (Discussion with author, August 8, 2008).

What Is the Background of the IAF's Work with Schools?

The Industrial Areas Foundation was begun by legendary community organizer Saul Alinsky in Chicago seventy years ago. Since that time, his original methodology has been adopted and modified across the world, and now the IAF has over sixty organizations in the United States, Germany, and Great Britain. These groups, typically composed of religious congregations, community groups, labor unions and, more recently, public schools, have effectively engaged thousands of low- and-moderate income families in getting affordable housing built, creating access to jobs that pay a "living wage" with benefits, expand- ing naturalization and citizenship programs, and increasing public resources provided to support education.

These successes, and many others, were gained by IAF organizers and leaders in their member organizations engaging in thousands of individ- ual and neighborhood house meetings to discover issues of community concern, identify potential leaders, and, most importantly, develop rela- tionships. These, in turn, led to thousands of people participating in actions and negotiations with officials leading to community improve- ments and to the IAF becoming what they call a "university for adults" where people developed leadership abilities and the skills necessary to engage in public life.

In the early 1980's, after many Texas IAF leaders had identified the lack of resources in their local schools as a major concern, IAF organizations in Texas were successful in getting the Texas legislature to appropriate an additional $1 billion for schools in lower-income communities. The IAF subsequently found, however, that even though having adequate financial resources was critical for the success of a school and its students, more money alone was not enough to raise student achievement.

They then began to explore potential strategies for working collaboratively with individual schools that would have several components, including two key ones:

- Parents and school staff collaborating to build relationships so they could improve school culture and student achievement.

- Obtaining financial resources and other kinds of support for schools by parents and schools working in partnership with other local institutions who believe their communities' own futures are dependent on student success. (Skills, Murnane and Levy 87 and conversation with Carrie Laughlin, August 27, 2008)

How Did the IAF's Community Organizing Work with Schools Begin?

The IAF organization in Fort Worth (located in Tarrant County), called the Allied Communities of Tarrant (ACT), first began this new effort in 1986 after being asked for assistance by the principal of Morningside Middle School, located in a low-income neighborhood. Beginning with congregations giving regular public recognition of students (for school attendance, books read, and other signs of academic success), parents (for reading to their children) and teachers, ACT leaders worked with teachers and administrators to develop a strategy for developing parent engagement at the school. This effort resulted in the school going from ranking last in Texas state tests among Fort Worth's twenty middle schools to third from the top within two years. Two years after that the school was awarded the Texas Governor's Excellence Award.

Since that time, a version of the organizing process developed in this collaborative approach has been used in over one hundred Texas schools across twenty-one school districts. Fifty additional schools have used a similar model throughout other states in the Southwest. IAF has also been successful in getting millions of dollars earmarked by the Texas legislature each year for schools working with community organizations as part of a restructuring process.

What does this process look like?

THE ALLIANCE SCHOOLS

After an IAF organization is asked for assistance by a local school, organizers, IAF volunteer leaders, and teachers typically first begin to have individual meetings with parents who tend to be most active in the schools. These meetings often take place in parents' homes. The purpose of these visits is to uncover parent concerns, to learn what they might have energy to do, and to discover potential leaders, defined as parents who have some longer-term vision for themselves, their children, their community; who have some desire for their own self-development; and who have a network, no matter how small, of other parents who might respect their judgment.

The primary point of these visits is to develop relationships through having reciprocal *conversations*, as opposed to the way schools often relate to parents—which is through one-way *communication* (Alliance Schools Concept Paper 2003). These individual meetings are then followed by a series of "house meetings," where parents invite others, including teachers, to small gatherings at their homes, at the school library, at a church, or elsewhere. The point of these meetings is not to create a "gripe session" but, instead, for parents to share some of what they've said at the individual meetings and begin to develop a common vision of where they want to go.

The next step is often a neighborhood walk, or a "Walk for Success." During a Saturday afternoon, teachers, parents, IAF leaders, and students will go throughout the neighborhood in teams of two to visit parents (and, often, other community members). An elementary school might try to visit all their students during one or two neighborhood walks, while a secondary school might target students in one particular grade. In these prior-announced visits teams will learn what people think the strengths of the school are, what needs to be improved, and what they might be willing to do.

Following these walks, depending on what is learned in the visits, workshops might be held on how parents can coach their children, how to obtain scholarships, what curriculum is being taught. During this period of time and, in fact, from the beginning of the school/community organizing effort, parents also learn civic engagement skills, including how to organize and lead group meetings, developing knowledge about local political structures and their dynamics, and learning the art of negotiation and compromise. Teachers also participate in this learning process.

Next, larger parent assemblies can be held (sometimes with public officials present to respond to school and parent proposals) and collaborative action plans developed with the school to begin work on issues identified in the parent conversations. These issues have included getting officials to prohibit alcohol being sold near campuses, bringing health care services to local schools, pushing for traffic lights to be placed at dangerous intersections, gaining resources to create in-school parent centers (in some instances, connected to the school libraries).

This organizing process was able to replicate the success begun at Morningside in other schools.

The rate of students passing the TAAS (the Texas state tests) in Alliance Schools increased from 2000 to 2001 at more than double the rate for all students in the state. In 2002, the rate of students passing the TAAS continued to increase at a higher rate than for all other students (Alliance Schools Concept Paper 4).

The Annenberg Institute for School Reform in 2008 issued the results of a multi-year study on the effect of community organizing in schools. A portion of the study focused on the sixteen schools in Austin, Texas that are part of the Alliance Schools. It, too, found that students in those schools passed the TAAS at a higher rate than students at other schools. (Kavitha Mediratta et al 2008).

This same study highlighted the results of teacher surveys that credited the organizing efforts with improving school climate and culture, "particularly on parent and community involvement, sense of community and trust in schools, and communication among school faculty and parents" (Kavitha Mediratta et al. 7).

In addition, the study found that two-thirds of parents "reported that because of their involvement in organizing, they were more likely to engage in … observing their child's class, talking informally with their child's teacher, looking at data to assess their school's performance, and raising concerns with the school principal or district leaders" (Kavitha Mediratta et al. 13).

Sixty percent of parents said that because of their participation in organizing they had "higher goals and expectations for themselves and their families" (Kavitha Mediratta et al. 13). This finding is especially noteworthy considering research findings that parent aspirations for their children play a key role in students developing self-confidence, earning higher grades, and deciding to attend college (SEDL 33, 35, 36).

It's important to clarify that the explanation of how IAF develops Alliance Schools is not a "cookbook"—it does not always follow the exact steps described in this chapter. Each local situation is different, and how it is organized depends on the local situation and desires of local leaders.

In addition, IAF's organizing with schools is indicative of an old organizing adage that "all organizing is re-organizing."

The passage of the federal *No Child Left Behind Act* (NCLB) in 2001 and how it began to be implemented had a major impact on many of the school districts where Alliance Schools were located. "In many places it created a climate of fear among district staff, and when people are afraid they are less likely to take risks," said Carrie Laughlin from the IAF Southwest Interfaith Education Fund (interview with author, August 27, 2008).

By 2004, even though Alliance Schools were demonstrating that students were progressing at a more rapid pace than those attending others, some schools (though by no means all) began to scale back their connection to the IAF. The pressure of NCLB, increased testing demands by the state, turnover among school staff and parents, more district-mandated curriculums and programs, plus more centralized control (one district began requiring that principals could not be away from their campus without prior approval from the district office) all combined to push some schools to be more inwardly focused (Laughlin, Duran, Greco interviews).

Three years later, though IAF had been continuing to work with many schools, it also developed some additional strategies on a statewide and local level to respond to this changing climate. It, along with other allies (particularly teacher organizations) convinced the state legislature to create a committee to study the accountability system and its affect on Texas schools. And in local communities, a number of school districts began to realize that the inward focus had not brought them the desired results and requested the IAF's assistance in developing more parent/community engagement again.

After the defeat of two school bond measures in San Antonio and a public outcry following a public report labeling local schools as "drop-out" factories, superintendents from two school districts in San Antonio approached the local IAF organization about working with schools and parents after a four-year absence.

IAF leaders and organizers, after conducting over 150 individual meetings with parents, confirmed their initial analysis: "The problem was that relationships had broken down. There were few relationships between teachers and parents, none between schools and the community, and hardly any between parents and other parents," said Ramon Duran, Lead Organizer of Communities Organized for Public Service (COPS) (conversation with author, August 26, 2008).

Then, instead of beginning the Alliance School organizing process as they had before—one school at a time—a decision was made to try to deal with the large parent turnover issue by a superintendent calling together 29 principals, all whom were in some kind of "feeder school" relationship. They agreed to participate in a five-year effort to work with the IAF on a parent/community engagement process reflecting the central elements described earlier in this chapter.

A similar situation is taking place in Austin. After a local high school in 2007 became the first one closed by the state because of failing test scores, Austin Interfaith (which includes the local teacher's union as a member) and the superintendent agreed to initiate a parent/community organizing process at nine other schools—another high school and all of its "feeders" (Doug Greco in conversation with author, August 28, 2008).

IAF organizations in California have adopted and modified the Alliance Schools' approach in two areas—the Central Coast (Monterey, Santa Cruz, Watsonville) and in Southern California.

ACHIEVEMENT ACADEMIES FOR SUCCESS

Live Oak Elementary School outside of Santa Cruz, California is a school with a student population of approximately forty percent Latino, forty percent white, and twenty percent of a mixture of other ethnicities. The school joined the local IAF affiliate, Communities Organized For Relational Power In Action (COPA) in 2004, as part of an effort to engage parents and improve state test scores. After using some of the organizing elements in the Alliance Schools (which are, in effect, the basic organizing tools IAF uses with all its member institutions), parents worked with the school to develop on-site ESL instruction for adults.

After that success, Joaquin Sanchez, COPA Lead Organizer, said that parents began looking at the question, "We want our kids to do better than we are doing, and what more can we do to make that happen?" (conversation with author, August 15, 2008).

In response to that question, parents, teachers, administrators, and leaders from another IAF member organization, the Family Resource Center, began to plan a parent "Achievement Academy for Success," a series of workshops for parents that was designed to be a long-term strategy for improving parent engagement.

Sanchez explains that the academy is designed for leadership development, "and not just about giving information. It's about helping parents develop their thinking about their child's education trajectory and what is their role: parent to child, parent to other parents, and parent to teacher" (conversation with author).

The curriculum for Achievement Academy for Success is different from one you might find in many parent *involvement* workshops. The curriculum, created by COPA, parents and teachers, has a large focus on reflective activities and not on what Sanchez calls a "checklist mentality of what every parent is supposed to do."

Activities and questions raised in the Academy include:

- Keeping a journal of asking your children daily what they did and learned in school that day.
- What has this helped you to learn about your child?
- What is creativity? Why is it important? How is your child creative?
- How do you build a relationship with your child's teacher? What questions do you ask?
- How do I know my child is learning? What kinds of enrichment activities can I help provide?

COPA is now working with Live Oak School District Superintendent David Paine to expand the Academies to other schools in the district, as well as exploring other ways to engage families. Superintendent Paine says:

> "We need more parent engagement. The traditional methods of parent involvement don't get results in our communities. School staff complain that parents don't care, don't show-up for Back-To-School Night. We need to dig at the reason why—maybe they don't feel welcome, there's a language barrier. Without that connection you won't get the academic achievement you want." (conversation with author, September 16, 2008)

PRE-K TO COLLEGE CAREER PIPELINES

Robert Cordova is a veteran principal now at Harmony Elementary School in South Central Los Angeles, a school with ninety percent of the student population classified as English Language Learners. He says he began working with the IAF at a previous school after he realized that the parents who he felt were "bothering me and getting in my way only wanted to have a better, safer school" (conversation with author September 13, 2008).

After he began focusing more on having conversations and developing relationships with these "pesky parents" they were able to work together and pressure the city to fully fund reconfiguring a dangerous intersection next to the school—an issue that people had complained about for twenty years. After that success, he says, those same parents became his biggest supporters.

He then came to Harmony committed to parent engagement. Harmony is a year-round school with three separate "tracks." When he first arrived, parents shared their concern that there was no equivalent of summer school when each track was on vacation, unlike at schools on a traditional calendar. Parents, staff, and leaders of other local institutions, comprising a "core team" of leadership at the school, were then able to get the District to fund that extra academic support.

Harmony's core team next began to consider that his school did not really have a relationship with any secondary schools, and that sixty percent of his students were not graduating with a high school diploma. They began working to develop a "Career Pipeline" including feeder schools and universities. For example, graduate students at local colleges who are interested in increasing minority enrollment mentor secondary students in various subjects. Those older students then go to Harmony to tutor younger children.

Harmony is one of only three schools in the Los Angeles Unified School District that has achieved a ten percent gain in each of the past three years in state and federal assessments. He attributes much of that success to the school's parent engagement strategy developed with the IAF. "It all starts with having conversations with parents in a thoughtful way. I'm looking for leaders who want to create power to get something done. I'm looking for leaders who want to create a community of learners," he says (Conversation between Cordova and Ferlazzo, September 13, 2008).

When asked what his response is to administrators who say they don't have the time to engage parents and the community in a similar way, he says:

> I don't do this by myself. Parents are willing to do it, as are teachers.
> For whatever time I put in, the school and I benefit ten-fold …
> I tell them that you don't have the time because you're doing it by yourself. If you think you're Superman—good luck. When you're feeling overwhelmed, you have to do something different. (Conversation between Cordova and Ferlazzo, September 13, 2008)

Whose Energy Drives This Work and Who Initiates It?

The initiator of this kind of organizing with a school varies—sometimes it's the principal who requests the assistance of an IAF organization. Other times it might be parents of students who attend a local school and who belong to another group (a religious congregation, union, neighborhood association, etc.) who is already involved with the IAF. Or it might be local neighborhood residents who, while they might not have children attending the school at that time, are nevertheless concerned about and aware of the impact a school's culture can have on the surrounding community.

The most important issue, however, is whose energy drives it. As mentioned earlier, a key IAF organizing tenet is the "Iron Rule: Never do for others what they can do for themselves. Never." The number of faculty, staff, and administrators at any given school will always be tiny in comparison to the numbers of parents and other community residents in that neighborhood. The challenge is for staff and parent leaders to look within themselves, and to elicit from parents what goals and interests would create the internal motivation necessary to engage in the life of the school.

What Are the Roles of the Parents and School Staff in This Organizing Work?

The principal obviously has a key role in organizing work with schools. The IAF will not organize in a school without the principal's support. (Mediratta et al 33).

Al Mindiz-Melton spoke of his role as the principal of Zavala Elementary School in Austin, Texas this way, "In an Alliance School culture, the principal's function is to be a talent scout" (Sheridan 62). In other words, his job is to identify leaders and potential leaders in the school and community.

Mr. Melton's view of himself as a talent scout is similar to the role teachers, other school staff, and key parent leaders also take in this kind of work. They need to look at themselves like an organizer does.

Ernesto Cortes, the Director of the Southwest IAF and who was awarded what is commonly called one of the MacArthur Foundation's "genius" grants, describes an organizer's role in this way:

> Organizing is a fancy word for relationship-building. No organizer ever organizes a community. What an organizer does is identify, test out, and develop leadership. And the leadership builds the relationships and the networks and following that does the organizing. If I want to organize you, I don't sell you an idea. What I do, if I'm smart, is try to find out what's your interest. What are your dreams? I try to kindle your imagination, stir the possibilities, and then propose some ways in which you can act on those dreams and act on those values and act on your own visions. You've got to be the owner. Otherwise, it's my cause, my organization. (Rogers 17)

Parents are not seen as reactive "clients," "customers," or "volunteers." Instead, they are pro-active co-creators. A San Antonio parent, Juana Ortega, described her new role this way:

> [After the Alliance School Initiative] I saw myself in a different light. I didn't come into this school as just a volunteer. I came into this

school as a partner in my child's education … It's no longer just sending her to school and let's see what happens. It's how can I ensure that she is going to get a good education? I found out it's just not the teacher's responsibility ... I have to be held accountable for what my daughter learns, not just the teachers. (Quezada 21)

What Is the Purpose, Who Has Decision-Making Power, and What Kinds of Partnerships Are Developed in This Organizing Work?

PURPOSE

The IAF is clear that its purpose in working with schools is not only to encourage parents to do what has typically been considered school *involvement* activities, such as helping students with their homework or volunteering in the classroom. In addition to those results, the main focus of the organizing work is to develop a broad base of parents, teachers, administrators, and institutions that want to work collaboratively to support local public schools and the surrounding community.

One major strategy for making this happen is through developing social capital by developing trusting relationships between individuals and between institutions. All the aspects of the organizing process used— individual and house meetings, neighborhood walks, parent assemblies, etc.—are designed to bring people together (and to exchange their personal stories) who had not previously been in a relationship.

DECISION-MAKING

The IAF's emphasis on developing relationships and social capital helps ensure that the issues it will focus on come out of those trusting relationships. Dennis Shirley in his book "Community Organizing for Urban School Reform" quotes Yale education professor and author Seymour Sarason as suggesting that "forms of involvement in decision making are in some ultimate, practical sense less important for realization of the spirit of involvement than degree and quality of the mutual trust and respect characterizing that involvement" (Shirley 251).

An additional way that IAF maintains a democratic and cooperating decision-making process is by having a strict criteria for any issue it will focus its energies on. This criteria includes:

- *The issue must have a better than fifty percent chance of being successful.* The reasoning is that parents and institutions in lower-income communities do not need help to fail—the point of organizing is to succeed, and to build on each success to solve bigger issues.

- *The issue must be specific.* For example, instead of saying "We want better traffic safety in our neighborhood," it has to be "We want a traffic light on this particular corner." Being non-specific in discussions with officials is a guarantee of non-success.

- *The issue must be non-divisive within the IAF organization and its partners.* There are plenty of issues (public safety, adequate facilities) affecting the well-being of children that parents, school staff, and neighborhood institutions can agree on and which come out of the school/community organizing process. The point of organizing is to focus on those issues and not on ones which might split alliances (school prayer, for example).

PARTNERSHIPS

In addition to schools, their staff, and parents, other local institutions, particularly religious congregations, are considered important partners in this type of organizing effort. IAF and its member congregations are always clear that congregations are not pursuing any kind of sectarian agenda and do not proselytize in their organizing work with schools. Local religious congregations can be a source of much neighborhood social capital and studies have shown that connections to them have a positive effect on family stability and student achievement (SEDL 32). In low-income communities, congregations are often one of the few institutions where families have any kind of supportive connections. The kind of relationships that the IAF develops between schools and congregations clearly respect the separation of church and state.

Teacher unions are also often member institutions in IAF organizations, especially when they are working on parent engagement efforts.

What Are Some Potential Challenges in Starting and Doing Work Like This?

There are several key challenges to initiating and continuing community organizing work with schools. This section will highlight four of them, most of which could also be applied to the other examples described earlier in this book. Some of these issues were also described by Dennis Shirley in his book about the Alliance Schools, *Community Organizing for Urban School Reform* (Shirley 223-240).

TEACHER TIME CONSTRAINTS

Teachers, particularly in urban school districts, often find that it takes an extraordinary amount of their time and energy to just successfully manage and engage large numbers of students each day. The idea of adding home visitation, participating in a house meeting or a parents' assembly, or taking part in a neighborhood "Walk For Success" can seem overwhelming, especially to those teaching in secondary schools and seeing up to 150 students each day.

IAF provides training to teachers to develop parent engagement skills, including how to manage their time effectively. The fact that parents themselves and leaders of other local neighborhood institutions are working for its success alleviates some of the additional time pressure, and, particularly for secondary teachers, meeting groups of parents more in house meetings might alleviate some logistical issues. IAF has found that the real key in assisting teachers get beyond this concern is to see the parent energy at a house meeting or parent assembly, and to experience the significant difference it makes in their students.

In Texas, many participating schools were eventually able to hire a parent support specialist/liaison with part of the state funds allocated to Alliance Schools. This additional support also assisted teachers in their parent engagement efforts.

PARENT TIME AND ACADEMIC CONSTRAINTS

Many parents are also facing constraints, including time limitations, of their own. Single-parent families, where the parent is working long hours and managing a household on their own, and two-parent families where long hours are worked just to barely make ends meet, will be challenged to find time to engage in the life of their children's school. Language can be a barrier, as well as needing to relate to multiple teachers in a secondary school. Some parents might feel intimidated by some of the higher level content taught in high school and, in fact, many might feel embarrassed that their lack of formal schooling even makes helping with primary grade content difficult. In addition, immigrant parents might come from cultures where parent participation in schools is not only not encouraged, but is actually discouraged.

Connecting to multiple self-interests of parents is key to dealing with several of these issues. These interests can include not only directly assisting their children gain greater academic success, but also issues related to neighborhood safety, health care, and citizenship/naturalization/ ESL classes. In addition to those "concrete" self-interests, many parents might also be eager to participate for other reasons—wanting to meet other parents, or a desire to further develop their own intellectual capacity. By listening to these concerns, and by inviting parents to see that they are all connected and that they can begin to effectively respond to them by engaging in school, schools can help parents overcome some of these constraints.

In addition, the support they can get from other local institutions in which they participate, and which are also involved in these organizing efforts, can provide additional assistance. Finally, teachers can provide many other ideas on how parents can support their children's academic development at home—no matter what the family's school experience had been. These strategies can include parents asking "strategic" questions about their children's schoolwork, telling stories, and teachers incorporating parents' "funds of knowledge" into their lessons.

PARENT MOBILITY

Low-income families can move often because of the lack of affordable housing and job instability, and that results in a large student turnover in urban schools. Parents might move searching for a slightly better home, or a block where they feel a bit safer. If parents believe they might be moving in a year or two, then that expectation can reduce the amount of energy they might be willing to contribute to engaging in their local school. School staff, too, can be disappointed if they repeatedly put a considerable amount of time into developing relationships with parents and then see them leave after a short time.

Of course, one response could be to emulate the example mentioned in the first chapter when the school worked with parents and a community group to build high-quality affordable housing in their neighborhood to help provide a more stable living situation for families. A number of Alliance Schools have worked with housing groups and realtors to develop "housing fairs" on campus for parents and included follow-up support.

This problem also speaks to the importance of schools working with multiple institutions in an organizing effort. It is not unusual today for families to move away from neighborhoods but to continue their relationship with certain local institutions like a religious congregation. In this way, even though their children might no longer be attending the local school, parents can continue to support the organizing efforts.

FINDING AN IAF ORGANIZATION

This chapter is not a "cookbook" on how a school on their own can use community organizing to engage parents. It would be challenging for a school to do a project like this without being in relationship with an IAF organization or similar organizing group. (It should be noted, though, that even though there are other national organizing networks that have had success organizing with schools, none have as lengthy of a track record as the IAF.)

School leaders can contact the national IAF office (see the "Resources" section at the end of this book) to see if there is a local affiliate, or, if there is not, inquire if it would be possible to negotiate a contract to receive technical assistance. Schools can also explore potential relationships with other national institution-based organizing networks that have had experience organizing with schools, including PICO and the Direct Action Research Training Center (DART).

Community organizing offers schools another way to *engage* parents, and not just *involve* them. At the same time, it provides an opportunity for schools to reclaim their roots as neighborhood "anchors"—not only as places to educate students but also as centers to support and improve communities.

Afterword

The boy was stung by a plant he touched tentatively. Without his mother's admonition to hold it boldly, he might have decided to never touch a plant like that again.

Engaging parents in school, particularly in urban schools, is not an easy thing to do. Since countless studies demonstrate how effective such engagement is in enhancing student achievement, if it was easy to do then it's probable that most, if not all, schools would be doing it already.

If you are a parent or school staff member, and are reading this book to help you consider how to engage parents in school, the point of this fable is not to encourage you to step forward blindly and tomorrow start a wide-ranging parent engagement effort. Instead, the point is to encourage you to seriously explore it—putting time and talent into this exploration—and make it a priority. And to recognize that it may not be a smooth road forward, and to not let the inevitable bumps deter you.

Seymour Sarason pointed to education reform pioneer John Dewey in describing why parent (and community) engagement is important in his book *Revisiting the Culture of the School and the Problem of Change*:

> In invoking the name and work of John Dewey, we come to the status of parents and other community groups as constituents in the change process. Almost a century ago he understood in an amazingly clear way that all those who would be affected by the educational enterprise would in some way be part of it, not out of considerations of courtesy or as token gestures ... but because the goals of education would not be met unless they had the support of diverse constituencies. (Sarason 294)

As the first chapter stated, this book is designed as a compass and not a road map to help develop that kind of support.

Works Cited

Alliance Schools Concept Paper: Interfaith Educational Fund, 2003. <http://www.dallasareainterfaith.org/alliance.htm>.

Castro, Peggy. Email to the author. 8 Aug. 2008.

Clapps, Elsie. *Forward to Community Schools in Action*. New York: Viking, 1939.

Coleman, James. Equality of Educational Opportunity (COLEMAN) STUDY (EEOS), 1966 [Computer file]. ICPSR06389-v3. Washington, DC: U.S. Department of Health, Education, and Welfare. Office of Education/National Center for Education Statistics [producer], 1999. Ann Arbor, MI: Inter-university Consortium for Political and Social Research [distributor], 2007-04-27. doi:10.3886/ICPSR06389

Coleman, James. "Social Capital in the Creation of Human Capital." *American Journal of Sociology*, v. 94, Supplement: Organizations and Institutions: Sociological and Economic Approaches to the Analysis of Social Structure. 1988: S95-S120.

Cordova, Robert. Personal interview. 13 Sept. 2008.

Cowan, Genie. *Home Visit Project: Year 03 Evaluation*. Sacramento: California State University at Sacramento, 2001.

Doggett, Carolyn. Email to the author. 6 Aug. 2008.

Duran, Ramon. Personal interview. 26 Aug. 2008.

Epstein, Joyce. "School/Family/Community Partnerships: Caring for the Children We Share." *Phi Delta Kappan* May, 1995: 701-712.

Ferguson, Chris, et al. "The School-Family Connection: Looking at the Larger Picture." National Center for Family and Community Connections with Schools. Austin, Texas: SEDL. June 16, 2008.

Fong, Nancy. Email to the author. 11 Apr. 2008.

Greco, Doug. Personal interview. 28 Aug. 2008.

Hanifan, L.J. (1916) "The Rural School Community Center." *Annals of the American Academy of Political and Social Science*, 67: 130-138.

Jeynes, William H. "The Relationship between Parent Involvement and Urban Secondary School Student Academic Achievement." *Urban Education* Jan. 2007: 82.

Krashen, Stephen. "Free Voluntary Reading." <www.schoollibraryjournal.com/article/CA6367048.html>.

Larkin, Maribeth. Personal interview. 8 Aug. 2008.

Laughlin, Carrie. Personal interview. 27 Aug. 2008.

Leana, Carrie and Fritz K. Pil. "Social Capital and Organizational Performance: Evidence from Urban Public Schools." *Organizational Science* May/June 2006: 353-366.

Mediratta, Kavitha et al. *Organized Communities, Stronger Schools: A Preview of Research Findings*. Annenberg Institute for School Reform at Brown University. March, 2008. Final report to be published by Harvard Education Press, Fall 2009.

Middleton, Kelly. "Sending Teachers on Visits to All Homes." *School Administrator* Feb., 2008 <http://www.aasa.org/publications/saarticledetail.cfm?Item Number=9745&snItemNumber =&tnItemNumber=>.

Moll, Luis. "Change as a Goal in Educational Research." *Anthropology of Education Quarterly*. 18.4 (Dec., 1987): 300-311.

Moll, Luis, et al. "Funds of Knowledge in Teaching: Using a Qualitative Approach to Connect Homes and Schools." *Theory into Practice*. 31.1 (1992): 132-141.

Murnane, Richard, and Frank Levy. *Teaching the New Basic Skills*. New York: The Free Press, 1996.

Organizations and Institutions: Sociological and Economic Approaches to the Analysis of Social Structure. A Supplement to "Social Capital in the Creation of Human Capital." *The American Journal of Sociology*. 94 (1988): S95-S120.

Paine, David. Personal interview. 16 Sept. 2008.

Parent Engagement: Creating a Shared World. 2007 <http://www.edu.gov.on.ca/eng/ research/pushor.pdf>.

Purves, A. and W. Elley. "The Role of the Home and Student Differences in Reading Performance." *The IEA Study of Reading Achievement and Instruction in Thirty-Two School Systems*. Ed. W. Elley. Oxford: Pergamon. 89-121.

Pushor, Debbie. "Parent Engagement: Creating a Shared World." *Ontario Ministry of Education*. Jan. 2007. <http://www.edu.gov.on.ca/eng/research/pushor.pdf>.

Putman, Robert D. *Bowling Alone: The Collapse and Revival of American Community*. New York: Simon & Schuster, 2000.

Quezada, Timothy. "Faith-Based Organizing for School Improvement in the Texas Borderlands: A Case Study of the Texas Alliance School Initiative." *The School Community Journal*. Spring/Summer 2004. <http://www.adi.org/ journal/ss04/T%20Quezada.pdf>.

Ramirez, David, Yuen, Sandra, & Ramey, Dena. *Final Report: Longitudinal Study of Structured English Immersion Strategy Early-Exit and Late-Exit Bilingual Education Programs for Language Minority Students*. Volume 1. San Mateo, California: Aguirre International, 1991. <http://www.ncela.gwu. edu/ pubs/ramirez/longitudinal.htm>.

RAND Corporation. "The Impact of Educational Quality on the Community." 2008 <http://www.rand.org/pubs/documentedbriefings/2008/RAND_DB562.pdf>.

Riley, Richard. <http://findarticles.com/p/articles/mi_puca/is_200005/ai_4220020674/ pg1>.

Rogers, Mary Beth. *Cold Anger*. Denton: University of North Texas Press, 1990.

Rose, Carrie. Personal interview. 10 Mar. 2008.

Rothstein, Richard. *Class and Schools—Using Social, Economic and Educational Reform to Close the Black-White Achievement Gap*. Washington, DC: Economic Policy Institute and Columbia University, New York: Teachers' College Press, 2004.

Rothstein, Richard. Response to the "March of the Pessimists." 2006.
    <http://www.epi.org/webfeatures/viewpoints/200608_rothstein_finn/rothstein-
    response_to_finn.pdf>.

Sanchez, Joaquin. Personal interview. 15 Aug. 2008.

Sarason, Seymour B. Revisiting "The Culture of the School and the Problem of
    Change." New York: Teachers College Press, 1996.

Sebring, P., A. Byrk, and J. Easton. "Charting Reform: Chicago Teachers Take Stock."
    Consortium on School Research, University of Chicago, 1995.

Sheridan, Laura. "The Alliance Schools Project: A Case Study of Community-Based
    School Reform in Austin, Texas." Public Administration Program, Texas State
    University, 1996. <http://ecommons.txstate.edu/arp/139/>.

Shirley, Dennis. *Community Organizing for Urban School Reform.* Austin: University
    of Texas Press, 1997.

Smith, Robert. *The Parent Home Visiting Project.* DVD. Sacramento, California:
    Walsmith Productions, 2006.

Southwest Educational Development Laboratory. *A New Wave of Evidence: The Impact
    of School, Family, and Community Connections on Student Achievement.* Austin,
    Texas: Southwest Educational Development Laboratory, 2002.

Tuss, Paul. *Evaluation of the CAHSEE Home Visit Pilot Project.* Sacramento County
    Office of Education, Center for Student Assessment and Program
    Accountability. Nov., 2007.

Resources

- Larry Ferlazzo has begun a blog called "Engaging Parents in School" (<http://engagingparentsinschool.edublogs.org/>) that will provide additional resources and answer questions about the issues and projects raised in this handbook.

- The following websites and books can also provide more information on beginning efforts similar to the ones described in this handbook. Contact information for organizations or resources that have been mentioned already in the book are listed but not described.

PARENT/TEACHER HOME VISITS:

- The Parent/Teacher Home Visit Project <http://www.pthvp.org/>
- National Education Association: Teacher Research Spotlight—Home Visits <http://www.nea.org/teachexperience/homevisits08.html>: Several resources are described on this page of the nation's largest teacher's union.
- PICO Network <http://piconetwork.org/>
- Sacramento ACT <http://www.sacact.org/>

TECHNOLOGY AND FAMILY LITERACY:

- Larry Ferlazzo's website <http://larryferlazzo.com/english.html>
- Larry Ferlazzo's Websites of the Day blog <http://larryferlazzo.edublogs.org/>: New resources that are added to the website used by students and their families are described in daily updates on this blog. The blog also has articles and tips on how to easily integrate technology into education.
- Verizon Tech Savvy Award Winners <http://www.famlit.org/site/c.gtJWJdMQIsE/b.2180327/>: Verizon sponsors annual awards through the National Center for Family Literacy to organizations using technology to promote family literacy. This page describes and provides links to the award winners.

SCHOOL COMMUNITY GARDENS:

- National Gardening Association <http://assoc.garden.org/>: This is a large national organization that supports home and urban gardening. It has a specific effort that is designed to have every school in the country have a garden.
- Garden ABC's <http://gardenabcs.com/>: Accessible information on starting community and school-based gardens can be found at this community-based site.
- California School Garden Network <http://www.csgn.org/index.php>: Even though this site is geared towards California schools, the bulk of resources there, including lesson plans and research, can be applied at any school.

SCHOOLS AND COMMUNITY ORGANIZING:

- Industrial Areas Foundation <http://www.industrialareasfoundation.org/>
- One L.A.—IAF <http://onela-iaf.org/>
- *Teaching the New Basic Skills: Principles for educating children in a changing economy.* Richard J. Murnane and Frank Levy, 1996, The Free Press. Chapter One, "Preparing to Meet the Future." This chapter describes the IAF's organizing work at Zavala Elementary in Austin, Texas.
- *Community Organizing for Urban School Reform.* Dennis Shirley, 1997, University of Texas Press. Professor Shirley's book argues that school reform needs to recognize the role of parents and the broader community in shaping the educational experience of children, and describes the successes of the IAF's Alliance Schools.
- *Valley Interfaith and School Reform.* Dennis Shirley, 2002, University of Texas Press. Professor Shirley writes specifically about the IAF's work in Texas' Rio Grande Valley.
- *Constituents of Change: Community Organizations and Public Education Reform.* Kavitha Mediratta, et al., 2004, Institute For Education and Social Policy, Steinhardt School of Education, New York University. <http://steinhardt.nyu.edu/iesp.olde/publications/pubs/cip/ConstituentsofChange.pdf>
- *Organized Communities, Stronger Schools: A Preview of Research Findings.* Annenberg Institute for School Reform at Brown University, Kavitha Mediratta, et al., 2008. <http://www.annenberginstitute.org/pdf/OrganizedCommunities.pdf>

PARENT INVOLVEMENT/ENGAGEMENT

(Note that some of the organizations and resources listed here might fall more into the "involvement" model and not the "engagement" one. However, they all offer useful information for those trying to encourage more parent participation in schools.)

- Parent Involvement Matters <http://www.parentinvolvementmatters.org/index.htm>: The organization has a specific parent involvement program it has developed, and also has more general resources and materials available on its website.
- National Network of Partnership Schools <http://www.csos.jhu.edu/P2000/>: Begun by Dr. Joyce Epstein at John Hopkins University, this organization does research, highlights best practices, and works with schools and parents to enhance parent involvement.
- National PIRC (Parental Information and Resource Center) Coordination Center <http://www.nationalpirc.org/>: SEDL, a nonprofit research group that has done work on parent involvement (including some of which has been cited in this book) coordinates this United States Department of Education resource center to support parent involvement efforts.

- National Coalition for Parent Involvement in Education <http://ncpie.org/>: NCPIE is a coalition of national and local organizations that advocates for the support of parent involvement efforts in schools.

- National Parent and Teacher Association <http://www.pta.org/homepage.html>: The PTA has numerous resources and publications on parent involvement.

- FINE: The Family Involvement Network of Educators of the Harvard Family Research Project <http://www.hfrp.org/family-involvement/fine-family-involvement-network-of-educators>: FINE, among other resources, offers a free email newsletter on recent research about parent involvement in schools.

Index